Ten-Minute Plays
VOLUME VII
FOR MIDDLE SCHOOL: DRAMA
10+ Format

Ten-Minute Plays

VOLUME VII

FOR MIDDLE SCHOOL

· · ·

DRAMA

10+ Format

YOUNG ACTORS SERIES

Kristen Dabrowski

A Smith and Kraus Book

A Smith and Kraus Book
Published by Smith and Kraus, Inc.
177 Lyme Road, Hanover, NH 03755
www.SmithandKraus.com

First Edition: April 2006
10 9 8 7 6 5 4 3 2 1
Manufactured in the United States of America

Cover and text design by Julia Hill Gignoux, Freedom Hill Design

ISBN 1-57525-439-5
10-Minute Plays for Kids Series ISSN 1553-0477

CONTENTS

TO MY BEST MATES IN THE UNITED KINGDOM
for their encouragement and enthusiasm

INTRODUCTION

Ten-Minute Plays aims to score on many playing fields. This book contains twelve short plays. Each play then contains two scenes and four monologues. Add it up! That means that this book contains twelve plays, twenty-four scenes, and forty-eight monologues. There's a lot to choose from, but it's not overwhelming. The plays and scenes are marked clearly. Note that the text for the monologues is set in a different typeface. If you are working on a monologue and are not performing the play or scene as a whole, take the time to hear in your mind any additional lines or character responses that you need for the monologue to make sense.

Beat indicates there is a dramatic pause in the action. You will want to consider why the beat is there. Does no one know what to do? Is someone thinking?

Feel free to combine characters (so fewer actors are needed), change a character from male to female (or vice versa), or alter the text in any way that suits you. Be as creative as you like!

For each play, I've included tips for young actors and ideas for playwrights. Here's a guide to the symbols:

🎭 = tips for actors

✍ = ideas for playwrights

There's a lot to work with here. Actors, the tips are meant to give you some guidance and information on how to be an even finer actor. Playwrights, I've included a few of my inspirations and invite you to borrow from them to write your own plays.

At the end of each play is a section called "Talk Back!" with discussion questions. These questions are catalysts for class discussions and projects. The plays do not make moral judgments. They are intended to spark students to use their imaginations and create their own code of ethics. Even if you're not in school, "Talk Back!" can give you some additional ideas and interesting subjects to discuss.

Lastly, there are four extras in the Appendix: Character Questionnaire for Actors, Playwright's Checklist, Scene Elements Worksheet, and Exploration Games. Each activity adds dimension and depth to the plays and is intended to appeal to various learning styles.

Enjoy!

Kristen Dabrowski

BOARDING SCHOOL

4F, 1M

WHO

FEMALES   MALE
   Jocelyn   Michael
   Maura
   Polly
   Rose

WHERE An old boarding school for girls.

WHEN Night, present day.

🎭 Take your time with all your actions to increase the sense of suspense.

✍ Write a ghost story.

Scene 1: Unseen

JOCELYN: What do you expect to find?

POLLY: I don't know.

MAURA: I'm not sure this is a good idea. What if we get caught?

JOCELYN: We'll pretend to be lost or sleepwalking or something. Nothing really bad will happen. Maybe we'll get detention. Big deal.

POLLY: Maybe we'll be famous.

MAURA: What do you mean?

POLLY: Maybe we'll get some respect. We'll show we're not just the little dorks they think we are.

MAURA: Who's "they"?

JOCELYN: Don't be stupid, Maura; you know exactly what Polly means. The popular girls.

MAURA: I don't care about them.

POLLY: Yes, you do. Everyone does.

MAURA: You think they'll like you because you go into the forbidden wing of the school.

POLLY: Yes.

JOCELYN: Definitely. Maybe. It's possible! It's *forbidden*, Maura. People will be talking about it. They'll want to know the story, so they'll *have* to talk to us and get on our good side.

MAURA: I'm not sure about this. What if . . . what if we *do* find something here? Something we shouldn't see?

POLLY: What? This place burned to a crisp years ago. There'll just be burned furniture and stuff.

MAURA: It has to be forbidden for a reason. You know what people say.

JOCELYN: A ghost. So what? A ghost is transparent. What could it possibly do? It's dead.

POLLY: It could scare you.

JOCELYN: If you let it.

POLLY: I don't believe in ghosts.

JOCELYN: Me either.

MAURA: But maybe it's dangerous. Maybe a beam will fall down from the ceiling or something.

JOCELYN: Well, if that happens we'll get help.

MAURA: Will you? Or will you be too afraid you'll get in trouble?

JOCELYN: Give us a little credit, Maura.

POLLY: Let's just do it. I'm getting more nervous standing around. The more we talk about it and wait, the more likely it is that we'll get caught.

JOCELYN: Come on, Maura. You first.

MAURA: This was your idea, Jocelyn! I really don't know why people like to be scared. I admit it! This freaks me out. I'm not sure I believe in ghosts, but I'm not sure I don't believe in them either. This could be something totally beyond our—I don't know. It just sounds stupid. It's not worth it to just get in with a group of mean girls. I have a really bad feeling about this. It's spooky here. And the girls who died here, trapped in a room, burning to death while they were alive, screaming and clawing to get out—well, I'd be upset if it were me. I might want to hurt someone or get revenge or something. I can't even think what that might be like. Can you imagine dying now, at our age? It's wrong. All this is wrong. I don't get why you want to do this. I'm not doing this. I'm going back to my room. And don't say I'm chicken. I'm not. I'm intelligent. And anyway, if we're going in, *you* should go first!

POLLY: Shhh! Keep it down!

JOCELYN: Fine. Just leave. Go back to the dorm room by yourself in the dark. I don't care.

(MAURA thinks.)

MAURA: You first.

JOCELYN: No. You.

(There's a standoff at the entrance between MAURA and JOCELYN.)

MAURA: Fine! I'll go. I guess we know who's chicken now.

POLLY: You!

(MAURA, POLLY, and JOCELYN enter a room.)

JOCELYN: Come out, come out, wherever you are!

MAURA: Jocelyn!

JOCELYN: You're wrong about me, Maura. I like to be scared. It feels delicious. I've got goose bumps! Come see, Polly! There's nothing like the adrenaline rush of cold fear. It's one of the best feelings in the world, right? I hope blood starts to drip from the walls. *(Beat.)* You know the story of this place, right? This room burned down with a bunch of girls in it. They were peacefully sleeping in their beds when a wacko maid who was jealous of them set it ablaze. They tried to get out, but the room was locked from the outside. They screamed and screamed, but no one could get them in time. Burned to a crisp. And now they're haunting this very room, hoping to finally get out before the flames set their nighties on fire. Delicious! Come on, girls. We're here to save you! Come out of hiding!

(A noise is heard.)

JOCELYN: Girls? Is that you? We mean you no harm. Really. So . . . Just don't hurt us. Please?

(A noise is heard.)

POLLY: Oh my God. See what you did, Joc? You made

them mad! We're going to burn to death, too! I bet they want revenge. I would!

MAURA: Shut up, you guys! Let's just go!

POLLY: I bet we're locked in.

(A creaking sound is heard.)

JOCELYN: Oh God! We're going to die here!

MAURA: Shut up! It's probably just the room. It's old. It creaks.

POLLY: She's right!

JOCELYN: We have to do this. It's important. We need to do something really big. In fact, I think we *should* get caught. In fact, I think we should spend the night in here. We have to prove ourselves. I'm sick of being a loser. I'm not a loser. I wasn't at my last school. So what if I'm not rich? It doesn't matter. And I'm going to prove it. I don't know what you two are going to do, but I'm staying. I want to get in trouble. I want to get a reputation as the girl who stayed in the ghost room. How cool is that? Come on, Polly. Stay with me. You can do it. Think about the rewards. Think about Beth, nasty Beth, begging you to tell her the spooky story again. And we can add stuff to make it more exciting! Only we have to agree on it so it seems true. *(Beat.)* Maura, don't you dare get me into trouble or tell on us. I want them to realize I'm missing in the morning. I want them to worry about where I am. I'm not going to be invisible anymore.

(ROSE rises up from behind some furniture and stands silently.)

POLLY: Is that you, Maura?

(MAURA reaches out to grab POLLY's arm.)

POLLY: Oh my God.

(Long beat while MAURA, POLLY, and JOCELYN stare at ROSE and try to master their fears and figure out what to do.)

POLLY: I'm sorry. I totally believe in ghosts. Don't be mad, please! Don't hurt us.

JOCELYN: Let's get out of here!

(POLLY and JOCELYN run out. MAURA is frozen in fear and stands still for another long beat.)

Scene 2: Untold

MAURA: Are . . . Are you a ghost?

ROSE: Almost.

MAURA: Almost?

ROSE: I'm alive, but I'm a ghost.

MAURA: How . . . ?

ROSE: I live here. I almost died here. They keep me here so I don't scare anyone.

MAURA: You were in the fire?

ROSE: Yes.

MAURA: And you live here alone? Does anyone know?

ROSE: They all know. Well, some of the teachers and the headmistress. They come and teach me sometimes. Oh, and Mrs. Glenn, the housekeeper. She comes in here sometimes. But I don't think she wants to. She's scared. I think she thinks I'm a ghost. I don't know why. I make enough real messes; you'd think she'd figure it out.

MAURA: But why . . . ?

ROSE: Do I live here? My parents can't take care of me. They don't have the money. And I guess the school feels responsible.

MAURA: I don't know why the school keeps you here. You seem fine to me.

(*MAURA begins to walk closer to ROSE.*)

ROSE: Don't come any closer! I don't want you to see my burns. I'm ugly.

MAURA: I'm sure you're not.

ROSE: I was even before the fire. Now I'm even uglier. At least it keeps most of the kids away. The smart ones anyway. Did you come to stare? Have a laugh? Because you can go now.

MAURA: No! I was here because . . . because those other girls wanted to come.

ROSE: So why don't you go?

MAURA: OK. I'm sorry. I didn't mean to— I hope I didn't—

ROSE: You didn't.

(*MAURA backs up to the door. As she does, MICHAEL enters with a bag, scaring MAURA.*)

MAURA: No!

MICHAEL: What?

MAURA: I'm going now!

MICHAEL: How did you get in here? Who are you?

MAURA: Who are you?

ROSE: My brother, Michael.

MAURA: Oh. Well, I got in through the door. And I'm Maura.

MICHAEL: What are you doing here? Every year some stupid girl tries to break in here to see ghosts. Most of them are smart enough to run away.

ROSE: That's what I told her.

MICHAEL: So you can get lost now.

MAURA: I'm sorry. I really am. I didn't mean to upset you.

MICHAEL: Yes, you did.

MAURA: No! Really! And . . . and if I can help you two—

MICHAEL: Don't worry about us. We're fine.

MAURA: I just thought if you have to hide . . . I could help you get stuff maybe.

MICHAEL: You want to help us.

MAURA: Sure.

MICHAEL: Why? Because you feel sorry for us, all cooped up in this room?

MAURA: Well . . . yes.

MICHAEL: We don't need your pity.

MAURA: That's not what I meant. Listen, I know you have every reason to be angry, but I didn't do anything to you—

MICHAEL: Except break into our room.

MAURA: It was open!

ROSE: Keep quiet! Both of you! *(Beat.)* No one can know we live here. It's the only way we can survive.

MAURA: So are you going to kill me or something?

ROSE: No! You just can't go blabbing. And we don't need your help. You'd just attract attention to us. But maybe . . . maybe you could meet Michael sometimes. It's not his fault I'm a monster.

MICHAEL: Rose, you're not a monster.

ROSE: And no one wants to have anything to do with me, not even my parents.

MICHAEL: Rose, don't be like that.

ROSE: It's the truth.

MICHAEL: Well, I'm here.

MAURA: I'm here, too, if you'll let me. I won't tell anyone. And I'll be careful. If you'll just—

MICHAEL: You're curious. That's all. Once you hear what you want to hear, all the gory details, you'll disappear. We don't need you.

MAURA: Please, why are you so mean? Can't you just give me the benefit of the doubt?

MICHAEL: Why?

MAURA: Well . . . I don't know who I'd tell anyway. I'm not popular, and people don't listen to me much anyhow. To be honest, I don't think I'd believe this story if someone told it to me. Everyone will think I'm lying. I'm not exactly the bravest, most daring person. The idea that I stayed and talked to you guys . . . well, no one would believe it.

MICHAEL: But you are talking to us.

MAURA: Yeah. I don't know . . . I feel like maybe we might . . . I don't know . . . have some things in common.

MICHAEL: What in the world would we have in common? We're prisoners, we're trapped, we're alone, we're in hiding, she's burned—

MAURA: I know! I don't mean all of it. I'm just . . . I don't want to sound like a jerk and like my situation is just like yours. It's not. I don't know what it's like to go through what you've gone through. Especially you, Rose. But I feel alone a lot, too. Outside of things. It sounds corny, but it's the truth. And at least you two are honest about it. Everyone else tries to pretend like they're happy, even if they're not. At least you're honest. This is the best conversation I've had all year. Sad, but true.

(MICHAEL smiles a little, despite himself.)

MICHAEL: Well, me too.

ROSE: Thanks a lot.

MICHAEL: Come on, Rose. You know we're both sick of each other. It might be nice to have someone else around sometimes.

ROSE: You changed your tune quickly.

MICHAEL: I don't know. I just got to thinking about our lives. We'll always stick together, but is this what the whole rest of our life will be like? We've got a lot of years together, Rose, maybe we should figure out how to deal with the world.

ROSE: You can leave any time you want.

MICHAEL: I know I can. But I don't want to. And I won't. *(Beat.)* You've got to give her credit, Rose. She's stuck around this long. No one else has lasted more than ten seconds.

MAURA: I really do mean what I said. I'm telling you the truth.

MICHAEL: I believe you.

MAURA: You do?

MICHAEL: Yeah. I don't exactly know why, but I do.

MAURA: Rose, please let me stay. Let me visit sometimes. I really don't mean you any harm. And I might be able to help sometimes. Oh! I've got chocolate! I stole it at dinner tonight. Want it?

MICHAEL: We could share it.

MAURA: Great.

(*MAURA breaks the chocolate into three pieces, keeping one and giving one to MICHAEL.*)

MICHAEL: Give me the other piece, too.

MAURA: No.

(*MAURA nervously walks over to ROSE and hands her a piece of chocolate.*)

ROSE: It's worse than you thought.

MAURA: No!

ROSE: I can see it in your eyes.

MAURA: No!

ROSE: You're a liar.

(*Beat.*)

MAURA: It's just the first time I saw you. So I didn't know what to expect.

ROSE: Well, now you know.

MAURA: Yes. (*Beat.*) Does it hurt?

ROSE: A little. Not so much. Not on the outside anymore.

MAURA: Oh. You must feel so isolated here. It's not fair.

MICHAEL: It's just the way it is.

MAURA: Does it have to be? I mean, once the other kids get used to seeing you—

ROSE: Please. You said that *you're* an outsider. And you're normal looking. And you think they'd accept me?

MAURA: Sure. Maybe even more than me. At least you're interesting.

ROSE: No. They'd make fun of me. I know it. They made fun of me before I was burned and it would only be worse.

MAURA: I understand why, I really do, but you're really negative.

ROSE: It easy for you to judge.

MAURA: I know. I just can't help thinking—

MICHAEL: Don't. I learned to stop thinking a long time ago. It's for the best.

MAURA: But I bet you didn't think you be talking to me tonight, did you?

MICHAEL: No.

MAURA: And you are. There might be other surprises out there for you.

MICHAEL: Maybe. But I think this is all I can handle right now.

MAURA: OK. Do you think I could come back tomorrow? I could bring some food.

MICHAEL: More candy or something? Because Mrs. Glenn only brings us healthy food. It's awful.

MAURA: Sure. Sounds good.

(Beat. *During the following dialogue, ROSE gets increasingly jealous as MAURA and MICHAEL get friendlier and more at ease.*)

ROSE: Give me a break. You're going to go back to your friends and either forget all about us or tell a story about the hideous freak you met tonight.

MAURA: No, I won't.

ROSE: Yes, you will. You don't know me. If you did, you'd never think we'd be friends. I don't have friends.

MAURA: What about your brother?

ROSE: He thinks he has to be my friend.

MICHAEL: No, I don't.

ROSE: Please. No one knows me. No one knows the real me. I don't deserve to be alive.

MICHAEL: Stop, Rose. That's not true.

ROSE: It's not? **Maybe I should finally tell you the whole truth. Then you can go off and be happy with your girlfriend here forever and finally leave me alone.**

MICHAEL: What are you talking about?

ROSE: I did it. I set the fire. It was all my fault. The girls in the room, my roommates, I hated them. They were cruel to me. All the time. So I wanted to die. And I wanted them to die with me. But they died, and I didn't. I heard them scream, and there was a moment when I wanted to take it all back, but I couldn't. I couldn't move. I was trapped. So I had to keep listening, and now I have to live with it. I'm a monster on the outside now, too. I deserve to be alone, uncared for. I deserve to be tortured. I deserve all of it. I'm a terrible person. I'm not even a person. I wish I were dead. I wish I never existed. You should just go, both of you, and leave me here. Or maybe I should go. Go somewhere to die.

MICHAEL: Rose—

ROSE: Now you know the real me, Michael. I've kept you trapped in this tomb with me all this time, and you never knew. You never did anything to me but be nice. And I made you a prisoner here with me. I'm sorry, Michael. I'm a terrible person. I hate myself. But I'm a coward. I couldn't tell you the truth. I couldn't be alone. I was scared. I'm so sorry. I understand if you want to leave. You should leave.

MICHAEL: Rose . . . I don't know what to say. I can't believe you'd . . . Is this the truth? You set the fire?

ROSE: Yes.

(Beat.)

MICHAEL: Oh God, Rose, why didn't you ever say . . . ?

ROSE: I was scared of being alone. I was scared you'd hate me. You hate me now, don't you?

MICHAEL: No. No. I just can't believe . . . *(To MAURA.)* You should go now.

MAURA: But—

MICHAEL: You should go now.

MAURA: I'll see you tomorrow?

MICHAEL: No. No. Don't come back.

MAURA: Why?

MICHAEL: Rose and I need to be alone. We shouldn't deal with other people. This is how our life is supposed to be.

MAURA: But I can help.

MICHAEL: I'll take care of Rose. I always have and I always will. We don't need anyone else.

MAURA: I don't understand.

MICHAEL: Don't tell anyone about anything you saw or heard tonight.

MAURA: I wouldn't.

MICHAEL: I mean it. Now go.

(Beat.)

MICHAEL: Did you hear me? Go!

(Beat. MAURA decides to go and walks out of the room, leaving ROSE and MICHAEL together in silence.)

TALK BACK!

1. Do you think Maura came back later? Would you?

2. Do you believe in ghosts? Why or why not?

3. What should you do if you see someone who is disfigured? You shouldn't stare, but you shouldn't ignore them either. So what is the right way to behave?

4. Have you ever thought of doing something destructive? Why do you think people do violent, destructive things?

5. Should Maura tell anyone what she knows?

6. Why do people take dares?

7. Why do some people care about popularity and being liked so much? How far would you go to be accepted?

8. Do you think Rose is being punished enough since she's disfigured and a prisoner, or should she be punished in another way?

9. Is Rose to blame for her actions all those years ago? Or was she justified?

10. Should Michael leave Rose?

NOON

1F, 2M

WHO

FEMALES   MALES
    Kit   Bobby
                            Marco

WHERE   A city. Scene 1: Outside; Scene 2: An old bridge.

WHEN   Present day.

Build an imaginary relationship between these characters. How do they know each other? How long have they known each other? Why do they hang around each other?

Write a play about revenge.

Scene 1: Revenge

KIT: *(To the audience.)* It was cold for August, meaning my shirt wasn't sticking to me yet, even though it was noon. I should have known that things weren't right that day. It was the day I swore for the first time. It was the day my father died right in the middle of the street. Shot. And I swore to kill the boy who did it. And I will. Today. In the middle of the street. Kill him just like he did to my dad. So I wouldn't stand around here if I was you. It's not safe. I'm not safe. I'm bound to do anything. I don't even know half of what I'm capable of. You'd be the same if it happened to you. Trust me on that. I know you can't really tell because it didn't happen to you; it happened to me. You should be glad about that. But all the same, I'm in a dangerous mood. I'm twitching for revenge. When I pull the trigger, I'm not going to stop until there's nothing left—no bullets, no sound, no nothin'.

(BOBBY enters.)

BOBBY: Kit, who you talkin' to?

KIT: Nobody.

BOBBY: You sure are actin' strange.

KIT: So what if I am?

BOBBY: I'm just sayin'.

KIT: Well, maybe you should stop sayin'.

BOBBY: Fine. Let's do somethin' then.

KIT: I am doin' somethin'.

BOBBY: What? You're not doing nothin'.

KIT: I'm waiting, ain't I?

BOBBY: For what?

KIT: Nobody.

BOBBY: If you ask me, that's just crazy.

KIT: I'm not crazy.

BOBBY: I'm not sayin' you're crazy, I'm sayin' you're actin' crazy.

KIT: You sound like your ma.

BOBBY: Don't say that. I ain't no woman.

KIT: Never said you was.

BOBBY: Better not.

KIT: Or what?

BOBBY: Or nothin'. *(Beat.)* Why we sittin' here? I thought you never wanted to come past here no more.

KIT: I changed my mind.

BOBBY: It looks different. New signs in the window of the shop.

KIT: Like I care.

BOBBY: Want an ice cream? Damn, it's hot today. My shirt's stickin' to me and it's only eleven-fifteen.

KIT: I think it's cold.

BOBBY: No way. It's hot.

KIT: I think it's cold.

BOBBY: You sure are actin' strange. Why're you so serious? 'Cause we're in front of your dad's old store?

KIT: Maybe.

BOBBY: We could go somewhere else, like I said. We could go grab a drink.

KIT: You go. I'm gonna wait.

BOBBY: For nothin'.

KIT: That's right.

BOBBY: Is this a girl thing?

KIT: It's got nothin' to do with girls.

BOBBY: If you say so. Well, I'm thirsty. Catch you later?

KIT: Sure.

(BOBBY exits. MARCO enters.)

MARCO: Shouldn't you be somewhere else?

KIT: Are you telling me to go?

MARCO: This isn't your neighborhood anymore, little girl.

KIT: Who says?

MARCO: Your brain should say so.

KIT: It don't.

MARCO: It should. Didn't you learn anything from your daddy?

KIT: I learned that life ain't fair.

MARCO: You can say that again. Now get lost.

KIT: I'm waitin'. And I ain't hurtin' no one.

MARCO: It's not that you're hurtin' anyone. It's that someone might hurt you. Take the fact that you're sitting out here in front of your father's old store . . . They might take that the wrong way. Like a challenge.

KIT: Maybe it is.

MARCO: Don't say that, Kit. Don't say that. You're scarin' me.

KIT: You're no one to me. You don't need to worry.

MARCO: You're my friend, right?

KIT: You ain't spoken to me in years.

MARCO: We grew up together. I'm allowed to worry. Just because we don't talk no more . . .

KIT: Just because we don't talk no more don't mean you get to worry about me. Mind your own damn business.

MARCO: And what if I don't?

KIT: Suit yourself then. I don't care.

(MARCO sits down next to KIT.)

MARCO: So, what're you up to, kid?

KIT: I'm not a kid. Not any more.

MARCO: Sure, you are.

KIT: Please. You need me to show you my bra?

MARCO: That's not what I mean. You're a kid on the inside.

KIT: What do you know? It's not like you're an adult. You're one year older than me. That's nothin'.

MARCO: Maybe so, maybe not.

KIT: Why are you talkin' to me?

MARCO: Why are you so angry?

KIT: 'Cause you're talkin' to me!

MARCO: Take it easy. I just don't think it's healthy for you to be here.

KIT: You made your point, OK? Let it go.

(Beat.)

MARCO: You're right.

KIT: I know I'm right.

   (Beat.)

KIT: What am I right about?

MARCO: You don't look like a kid. No one else's gonna think you're a kid.

KIT: Probably 'cause I'm not, Marco.

MARCO: Polo.

KIT: Ha, ha. Very funny.

MARCO: Just doin' it before you did.

KIT: I wasn't going to.

MARCO: Sure you were.

KIT: You don't know me no more, Marco.

KIT/MARCO: Polo!

MARCO: See? I told ya so. *(Beat.)* Who ya waitin' for?

KIT: Guy that killed my dad.

MARCO: You're jokin', right? Tell me you're jokin', Kit.

KIT: No joke.

MARCO: You're scarin' me. Really and truly. What do you think you're gonna do?

KIT: I think I'm gonna kill him like he killed my daddy.

MARCO: No. No, you're not.

KIT: Yes, I am. Watch me.

MARCO: I won't. *You* won't. We're outta here.

KIT: I'm not goin' nowhere.

MARCO: You're comin' with me, Kit.

KIT: No way. You can't make me.

MARCO: Sure I can.

KIT: No you can't!

MARCO: What are you gonna do—shoot me?

KIT: Maybe I will.

(Beat.)

MARCO: Come on, Kit. Come with me. Forget this.

KIT: I can't forget this. I'll never forget this.

MARCO: I mean this idea you got now. Forget it. Come on. Let's go. We'll do somethin' fun.

KIT: I'm on a mission, Marco. You couldn't understand.

MARCO: I do understand. I understand completely. Now let's go!

KIT: How do you understand?

MARCO: I know someone who died. Last year. They shot him in the belly. He died real slow. Bled to death. It was terrible. This guy, he wasn't always good. It's hard to be around here. It's hard to stay out of things. But if you could have seen him, heard him askin' for his mother . . . Whatever he done he was sorry for. And nothin's worth what he got. All this's gonna keep goin' on and on and on if someone doesn't stop it.

KIT: I won't be the one to stop it. I need my revenge.

MARCO: No, you don't. Revenge is no good. You'll be sorry when you're watchin' this guy you shoot cough up blood and there's parts of him stuck to your clothes and you see his brother or his daughter cryin' over his dead body. You'll be sorry when the police take you away—

KIT: I won't. I'll be happy.

MARCO: Please, Kit. Let's go somewhere. Please.

KIT: Where?

MARCO: Anywhere.

KIT: If you can't even tell me—

MARCO: Anywhere. Anywhere you want. Let's just go.

KIT: If I go, I'm comin' back later.

MARCO: OK. OK. Just for now, then. Let's go.

Scene 2: Regroup

MARCO: Why did you want to come here?

KIT: Dunno.

MARCO: It's high. Maybe we shouldn't be here.

KIT: Are you a man or a mouse?

MARCO: Don't start with me. I don't like heights, that's all.

KIT: What are you scared of?

MARCO: Fallin', of course.

KIT: You ain't gonna fall.

MARCO: You don't know that. You—you wouldn't push me would you?

KIT: Why would I do that?

MARCO: I dunno. People are crazy.

KIT: I'm not crazy. You think I'm crazy?

MARCO: No, no. It's just . . .

KIT: High.

MARCO: Yeah. I dunno. Got a thing about heights.

KIT: You'll be OK. Just sit for a while. I'm going back to the store soon anyway.

MARCO: OK. I'm gonna be fine. Not gonna fall. Gravity doesn't exist.

KIT: Here I am thinkin' you're a tough guy all this time. You're a marshmallow.

MARCO: Am not. You better believe that if I needed to—

KIT: You'd shoot somebody?

MARCO: No. Not that.

KIT: What then?

MARCO: I'd take care of myself and the people around me.

KIT: By shooting someone.

MARCO: I told you, I had it with that.

KIT: So who was that guy?

MARCO: What guy?

KIT: The guy who was shot.

MARCO: Oh. My older brother.

KIT: Oh. You was close?

MARCO: Yeah. Well, sometimes. Sometimes not. He was my brother, you know?

KIT: Yeah, I know. So why'd he get shot?

MARCO: I guess the usual. He pissed somebody off, he fought with the wrong guy, maybe he even shot someone. I don't know.

KIT: Then he deserves it.

MARCO: No, he didn't! Take that back, Kit. I mean it. Take it back.

KIT: Well, maybe he shot somebody so maybe he shoulda been shot.

MARCO: No, he should be alive. You shoulda seen my mama this Christmas, cryin' and cryin'. That ain't right. That's not Christmas. Even if maybe he done some bad things, that don't mean he should die. And it don't mean my mama should suffer because of it.

KIT: What if who he shot was my daddy?

MARCO: It wasn't.

KIT: What if it was?

MARCO: Then too many people are already sad. No need to make more.

KIT: Why not? The police aren't getting justice. No one's stopping anybody. Maybe if they knew there would be revenge—

MARCO: But they do know. A lot of the time, they do know. My brother knew. He was lookin' over his shoulder every minute. That's no way to live.

KIT: But nobody thinks some girl's gonna do somethin'.

When that kid shot my daddy he didn't think somethin' was gonna happen to him. He just shot some dumb shopkeeper. But that was my dad.

MARCO: I know. It's wrong. But God will punish him.

KIT: And what if he doesn't? And what if he shoots another shopkeeper? Shouldn't he be stopped? I think he should. And I also think I will feel better after I do it.

MARCO: You won't.

KIT: You don't know that.

MARCO: I do.

KIT: How?

MARCO: 'Cause **I do know you. Better than you think. I know you like goin' to school—**

KIT: Not anymore.

MARCO: **—and talkin' to your friends—**

KIT: Everybody does.

MARCO: **—and cherry Italian ice that makes your lips and tongue all red and pictures of old movie stars and the color green and dumb comedies where people fart a lot—**

KIT: Like you don't.

MARCO: **—and your cousin Junie and goin' to the park**

and lyin' under the trees and sittin' on the edge of bridges, even though it's dangerous.

KIT: Chicken!

MARCO: Maybe. But I know a lot about you. I've seen you on the streets with your friends and your family. You're not so different from how you was when you were little. You're just sad and mad now, since your daddy's gone. But you're still a nice girl. You still like a lot of things you'd miss if you was in jail. And I know we never talk, but I'd miss seein' ya and hearin' that awful laugh of yours—

KIT: My laugh is not awful.

MARCO: **It's the worst laugh I ever heard. Sounds like you're drownin' a chicken. But it's funny, and I like it. So don't be crazy no more, Kit.**

KIT: I told you; I'm not crazy.

MARCO: You know what I mean. Let's be friends again, and I'll protect you.

KIT: You can't.

MARCO: I can try.

KIT: You can't bring my daddy back.

MARCO: No one can. But you can grow up and get outta here and go somewhere that *he* ain't and live happily ever after.

KIT: No such thing.

MARCO: Isn't it possible?

KIT: No. I don't think so. There's no happily ever after. I don't know why kids get told junk like that. At least kids around here. We ain't gonna see nothin' but death and hunger and violence. Things kids ain't supposed to see. Happily ever after 'round here means you eatin' from McDonald's dollar menu and your whole family comes home without holes in them. And you worry until they show up. And you half hate 'em for makin' you worry. And maybe you even had a fight with them and think you don't care if they come home. Nothin' happy about any of it. I don't know why anybody bothers. I don't know why anybody laughs. I don't laugh no more. There's no point. Everythin's bad. I don't even know why I go on livin'. I wish it was me that got shot and not my dad.

MARCO: Don't say that.

KIT: Stop tellin' me what to do and say and think!

MARCO: Your daddy was shot because maybe for some reason he was supposed to be shot.

KIT: What?!

MARCO: Maybe he was supposed to make you see how wrong it all is. Maybe otherwise you'd be in some gang right now and be in a bad place. Maybe you'd be pregnant and not know who the daddy is.

KIT: And maybe not.

MARCO: But maybe so. Maybe there's a meanin' we don't see.

KIT: And maybe the reason is I'm supposed to ice that other guy.

MARCO: I know that ain't it.

KIT: You can't know that.

MARCO: I do. You're supposed to stay here with me. And I was supposed to talk to you today. And we're supposed to be friends again. And maybe I'm supposed to take care of you from now on.

KIT: And maybe not.

MARCO: And maybe so.

(Beat.)

KIT: It's almost noon. It's time for me to go.

MARCO: No, Kit. Stay. I think I'm getting used to being so high. Maybe you got me over my fear of heights.

(BOBBY enters.)

BOBBY: Here you are. I thought I wasn't gonna find you.

KIT: Get lost, Bobby.

BOBBY: Your cousin Junie's lookin' for ya. Wants to know if you want to go to try on some tops or somethin'.

KIT: Well, you can tell her no.

BOBBY: Why?

KIT: Just no.

BOBBY: She's gonna ask me why.

KIT: I don't feel like it.

MARCO: Go, Kit.

KIT: Stop tellin' me what to do! Just no, OK?

BOBBY: OK, OK! You sure are actin' strange.

   (BOBBY exits.)

KIT: He bothers me sometimes.

MARCO: I noticed.

KIT: I gotta go.

MARCO: Kit—

KIT: I gotta go!

MARCO: Please, Kit. Don't.

KIT: I gotta go.

TALK BACK!

1. Can you understand how Kit feels? Why or why not?

2. What would you do if you were in Kit's situation? What do you think Kit will do at the end of Scene 2?

3. Why do you think Marco wants to stop her?

4. Fight fire with fire. Do you think this is a good motto or a bad one? Does violence create more violence?

5. Have you ever known someone who died before he or she was old? What was this experience like for you?

6. Do you think Kit will feel better if she gets her revenge? Why or why not?

CHANCE

3F

WHO
FEMALES
Alanis
Ariana
Quinn

WHERE Scene 1: The school locker room; Scene 2: Alanis's house.

WHEN Present day.

🎭 Make sure you decide exactly what's gone on between Scene 1 and Scene 2. What's changed for your character? How has Alanis's experience changed each character?

✎ I saw a story about an accident like this one on TV. It got me thinking about how I might react if it happened to me. Imagine that you lost one of the abilities you take for granted, and write a play about it.

Scene 1: Psyched

QUINN: I'm so nervous.

ALANIS: It's just another race.

QUINN: But my dad is coming today.

ALANIS: You'll do fine. You always do.

QUINN: No, *you* always do fine. I stink half the time.

ALANIS: You just need to stay focused and relaxed. Don't you get excited before a race?

QUINN: Never! I get sick.

ALANIS: I love that feeling of anticipation. Something's going to happen! And I'm in such a good mood today, so I'm double psyched for the meet.

QUINN: You're nuts. And you're good. So I guess it makes sense.

ALANIS: I can't believe you don't feel that way.

QUINN: Absolutely not. I'm about to puke.

ALANIS: If your dad sees you doing great, think of how amazing that will be.

QUINN: Yeah, but what if I do badly?

ALANIS: You look at things all wrong. Your dad is out there! You have support! How can it be bad?

QUINN: I guess the glass is half empty with me.

ALANIS: What?

QUINN: Whatever. Doesn't matter.

(ARIANA enters.)

ARIANA: What's going on?

ALANIS: Quinn's worried about her dad coming to the meet to see her.

ARIANA: I know what you mean. It's so scary, isn't it?

ALANIS: Why do you think that? I don't get you guys.

ARIANA: If I don't swim with the form my dad thinks I should have, he tells me about it over and over and over again until I wish I didn't swim at all.

ALANIS: I like it when my dad gives me tips.

QUINN: You're nuts. Seriously.

ARIANA: I hate it when my dad does that. It just makes me feel like I do everything wrong when he criticizes me. He wants me so badly to be good, and it has the exact opposite effect. I start to worry so much about form that I can't swim well. I go really slow because I'm thinking about the curve of my arm and stupid stuff like that. Then my dad is doubly mad at me and lectures me even more. Then I pay attention to going faster, and we're back at the beginning. It's an evil circle. I know he's trying to help, but it's awful. Don't parents realize they take all the fun and enjoyment out of things when they do that? Plus, we have coaches. Why do I have to have another coach at home? It makes you feel like you can never just rest. It's exhausting and stressful.

QUINN: I understand. My dad's not quite like that, at least about swimming, but I get it.

ARIANA: What's your dad like?

QUINN: Oh, well, my dad doesn't come to meets. He's always working. So, I don't know, when he does come to something, I freak out. I want so badly to be good and show him what I can do to make him want to come more. I don't see him so much at all, so it feels like a big deal when he does show up. Then when I stink at whatever he's come to see— a school play, a choir concert, a swim meet—I feel like I blew it and he's not going to come to anything any more. And it's kind of true. He'll say to me afterward, "Nice job" or something like that, but he says it like he'd say, "Nice weather we're having." So I know he's just being polite and my mom made him come. Then he doesn't come to anything again for a year or two. And during that year or two, I don't know, I start to really want his attention or something. Sounds stupid, I guess.

ARIANA: No, it makes sense. I know what you mean. But maybe you can be glad sometimes that your dad isn't all over you, picking on you and criticizing you all the time, like mine is.

QUINN: I guess. I guess that's bad, too. Why can't dads just be normal? Not too much attention, not too little.

ALANIS: I guess I'm really lucky. My dad and I get along so well. It's my mom I fight with. My dad and I are best friends practically.

QUINN: Oh, well, don't even get me started on my mom. She is so oppressive.

ARIANA: My mom is just a ditz, I swear.

ALANIS: My mom just really, really doesn't understand me. I guess she's nice and all, but we are two completely different people. For instance, she sits around all the time watching TV. And she'll actually say to me, "Alanis, why don't you just stay in the house a while and relax?" She'll say that when I'm about to go running or something. How sick is that? People are supposed to exercise. Most parents are trying to get their kids to be healthy and get out of the house more. What is she doing trying to make me slow down and stay in? Is she trying to make me fat or something?

QUINN: Who knows? Mothers are a mystery.

ARIANA: I think whatever you like and want to do, they think it's their job to think it's bad.

ALANIS: Well, it's dumb.

QUINN: I'm so depressed now.

ALANIS: Don't be! We shouldn't be talking about this.

ARIANA: What should we be talking about?

ALANIS: We should be talking about and thinking about

what we'll get after the game as a reward. Keep our eyes on the prize.

QUINN: I'll never win a prize, are you kidding?

ALANIS: Well, maybe not *the* prize, but we'll go out for pizza and have a party.

ARIANA: You'll win a prize for sure, Alanis.

ALANIS: But, see, that's just it. I can see myself swimming perfectly. I can see it clear as day. I can see each stroke, I can see other swimmers struggling to keep up, I can see myself reaching to the edge of the pool—I can see it all! You have to be able to see it to get it.

QUINN: I think the movie projector in my head is broken. Or moving in slow-mo or something.

ALANIS: That's because you're negative. You have to be positive. Try it for once. What's the worst thing that could happen?

QUINN: I still stink.

ALANIS: And you stink anyway! Well, you don't stink, but you think you do.

QUINN: I guess I could try.

ARIANA: I'll try it. What the heck.

QUINN: I bet I'll lose anyway, though.

ALANIS: You see everything so black and white. You either win or you're a loser.

QUINN: It's true, isn't it?

ALANIS: No! Thinking more positively won't make you a totally different swimmer, but it can make you better. And isn't better a good thing?

ARIANA: *(Shrugs.)* Eh.

QUINN: I still want to win.

ALANIS: Well, of course you do. And that's good. But you can't win 'til you get better.

ARIANA: You're so happy.

QUINN: It's kinda scary.

ALANIS: And you guys are seriously frustrating.

QUINN: What's new? You sound like my mom.

ALANIS: Thanks a lot.

QUINN: Well, it's true.

ARIANA: I guess we'd better get dressed. The meet is in fifteen minutes and you know the coach will want to talk to us beforehand.

ALANIS: I cannot wait!

QUINN: You are so demented, Alanis.

ALANIS: I am a winner!

ARIANA: Whatever. Good for you.

ALANIS: You'll see. I have a really good feeling about today. Everything's going to go right. I'm coming home with a prize!

ARIANA: You probably will. You're really good.

ALANIS: Listen, if anyone should be nervous here, it should be me. I've got the most at stake. If I win this, I'm going to states. So, please, don't make me nervous or worried. I want to be happy today.

QUINN: Sorry, Al. You know I didn't mean to do that, right?

ALANIS: Yeah, of course.

ARIANA: We love you! You're gonna do great!

ALANIS: I think I might.

ARIANA: Of course you will!

QUINN: It's your destiny to win.

Scene 2: Psyched Out

(ALANIS is sitting in a room, not moving for several beats. QUINN and ARIANA enter.)

QUINN: Al!

ARIANA: Hi, Alanis.

(Beat.)

ALANIS: You know you didn't have to come.

ARIANA: Of course we didn't have to come. But we did.

QUINN: We wanted to see you.

ALANIS: Well, now you saw me. Bye.

(Beat.)

ARIANA: So that's how it's gonna be.

ALANIS: I guess so.

QUINN: Are you mad at us? *(Beat.)* Did we do something?

ARIANA: We just wanted to see if you were OK; if there's anything we can do for you. Is that so bad?

QUINN: Do you think it's our fault? *(Beat.)* Sometimes *I* think that.

ARIANA: Quinn, don't be crazy. We didn't do anything, and Alanis knows it.

QUINN: But she was in a good mood and feeling confident before we showed up. Maybe somehow . . .

ARIANA: No, come on. That doesn't make any sense. You don't think that do you, Alanis?

(Beat.)

ALANIS: No, OK? So you can go now. You don't need to feel guilty. You didn't make me do anything. No one can make me do anything.

ARIANA: And no one, especially a friend, would wish something like this on another person.

ALANIS: "Something like this." You can just say it, Ariana. I'm a cripple. I'm useless.

ARIANA: You can't walk. You're not useless.

QUINN: Don't think that, Al. You're still the same person—

ALANIS: No, I'm not. I'm not the same person at all.

QUINN: I mean, who knows? You might be able to walk again sometime. With technol—

ALANIS: No, I won't. Don't be stupid.

QUINN: I'm not stupid.

ALANIS: If you say so.

ARIANA: Don't be a jerk, Alanis.

ALANIS: Don't be cruel to the cripple, Ariana.

ARIANA: Are you trying to get us to leave?

ALANIS: Did you just figure that out, Einstein?

ARIANA: Well, I certainly didn't come here to be treated like this. I don't care if you can walk or not. You're not allowed to be this mean to us. Let's go, Quinn.

QUINN: I don't wanna go. I wanna talk to Alanis.

ARIANA: Alanis isn't here.

ALANIS: Who am I then? This is the real Alanis.

ARIANA: Whatever. She's a bitch.

QUINN: Ariana!

ARIANA: What? That's how she's being. We came over here to be nice—

ALANIS: To see the cripple—

ARIANA: Will you shut up about the cripple thing!

QUINN: Ariana!

ARIANA: Well, it's stupid! No one's walking around saying, "Gee, that Alanis is such a stupid cripple now. Too bad she's not cool anymore 'cause she's a cripple." What kind of idiots do you think we are?

ALANIS: What are you saying then?

ARIANA: People are saying, "It's sad what happened to Alanis. I can't believe it. I hope she comes back to school soon." People like you, Al. We like you most of all. So don't push us away. It's like a dumb movie-of-the-week the way you're acting. I get it, really I do, I understand why, but don't be like this with us. We love you. We want you to get better. We don't care if you can walk. Really. I mean that. It's not B.S. It's serious. I'd be upset if something so freakish—not you, the accident—happened to me. It must be scary and sad and awful. But don't push us away. It's such a typical thing. And you are not a typical person, so just quit it.

ALANIS: What do you know?

ARIANA: I'm not pretending to know anything.

ALANIS: Sure you are. You're asking me to put on a happy face for you. Give me a break. A month ago I dove into a swimming pool to win a race that would send me to state championships, hit the bottom of the pool, and came out a cripple. Where's the happy face in that? News flash—there isn't one. It sucks. Every day of my life I have to be a freak. Every day! I don't get to wake up one day and feel better like when you get sick. Every day I wake up and try to get out of bed and I can't. Every day there's a new thing I realize I can't do. I need people's help to do, like, everything. Get a jar out of a cabinet, get dressed, go to the bathroom—can you imagine what that's like? To be like an infant again? To not be able to do practically anything yourself? To depend totally on your mother like a baby? It's terrible. And they hate me, my parents. They hate taking care of me. And I'm awful to them, and I can't help it. I'm a terrible person. It would have been better if I'd died.

QUINN: That's not true! It's not true. I know this must be hard—that's not even a good enough word to describe it—but you have to keep trying, Alanis! You'll need your mom less and less. You just . . . Oh, it's stupid for me to tell you what to do. I don't know what it's like. I can't even imagine. And I know we must sound like jerks. But . . . we really do just want to be your friends. We want you to be better. Do you think you can just, I don't know, talk to us again?

ALANIS: I am talking to you.

QUINN: You know what I mean. Like we're your friends.

ARIANA: We want to be your friends. You can tell us anything. You can tell us what's bothering you. You can tell us your mom is driving you crazy. You can tell us anything at all.

ALANIS: Wow. That sounds hunky-dory.

ARIANA: Why are you making this so hard? I know you must want someone to talk to other than your mom all day.

QUINN: Well, and her dad.

ALANIS: My dad doesn't talk to me anymore. He's disgusted with me.

QUINN: Why?

ALANIS: I'm a brat. I don't try hard enough. I don't appreciate what I have. I'm a terrible person.

ARIANA: That doesn't sound like your dad.

ALANIS: Well, it is.

ARIANA: You must be acting like a real pig.

QUINN: Ariana!

ARIANA: What? She must be or her dad would never be like that. I've never in my life seen a dad who was more supportive or nice. Ever. Her dad thinks she's the best thing ever.

ALANIS: He did. When I was winning awards and making him proud.

ARIANA: That's crap. For one thing, I seriously doubt he hates you now that you don't swim. That would make him, like, evil. And there are plenty of awards you can still win. So what if you can't swim? And you still have arms, anyhow. Can you really not swim?

ALANIS: Are you saying I should join up for the Special Olympics?

ARIANA: Maybe.

ALANIS: Please. I'd rather be dead.

QUINN: Don't say "dead" anymore!

ARIANA: You're too good for the Special Olympics? I

think you're the one with the problem with disabled people.

ALANIS: Oh, and you know all about it.

ARIANA: No, I don't. But I know enough to know that they deserve more respect than you're giving them. And you of all people should know they deserve it.

ALANIS: Because I'm a useless cripple, too?

ARIANA: Yes! OK? You can't walk. You're crippled. I'm not under any delusions about that.

ALANIS: Come on. Give me one more inspiring speech.

ARIANA: Shut up, Alanis.

ALANIS: I bet if I got just one more uplifting speech, I could get out of this chair.

ARIANA: Shut up.

QUINN: Maybe you could. I mean you're always the one who would talk about—

ALANIS: Quinn, you're a moron. You don't know anything. So maybe you should keep your big mouth shut.

QUINN: Oh. OK.

(Beat.)

ARIANA: Nice, Alanis.

ALANIS: Why don't you just leave now?

QUINN: You're the one who used to always say we should think positively and visualize what we want. See the goal. *You're* the one who said that. So, I don't know, maybe you should take your own advice. *Your* advice from before the accident. You thought you were right then. You thought you were smart. And you thought I was stupid for being negative. And now you think I'm stupid for being positive. You were never my friend at all, were you?

(Beat.)

ALANIS: I was. I . . . meant what I said then. And . . . I didn't say it to be mean. I said it to help. I never thought you were stupid.

ARIANA: So why did you say it?

ALANIS: I get it, OK? I said it to try to help. Like you're doing now. I get it. But it's not the same thing. A swim meet and being crippled for life. It's not the same! And maybe you were right all along, Quinn. Maybe everything is just fate and bad luck and maybe we're all just doomed. Maybe you were the smart one after all. You were. I was the idiot for thinking that if I could just imagine a happy life with everything going my way, it would happen like that. That's idiotic.

QUINN: No, it's not. I mean, it's not going to always go that way, obviously, but you have to think like that anyway, right? Or else what's the point?

ALANIS: This is stupid and sentimental. I'm not talking about this anymore.

QUINN: Why?

ALANIS: It's sappy. There's no happy ending for me anymore. Sure, I can live a full life. I can get better at doing things for myself. I can go to college. And I can be totally alone. I can have people staring at me for the rest of my life. I can look at people's groins forever instead of their eyes. Sure, I can keep living and I can act like one of those plucky people you see on TV and think, "Wow, she is so brave!" but I'm not really that person. That person is delusional.

ARIANA: But what's the fun in being sad all the time?

QUINN: You don't have to be alone.

ALANIS: 'Cause I have you? Pardon me for saying so, but please. Give me a break.

ARIANA: Well, I've had enough depressing crap and insults for today. You, Quinn?

QUINN: I guess so.

ALANIS: Well, good. Bye-bye. Don't let the door slam you in the butt.

ARIANA: We won't.

QUINN: See you tomorrow, Al.

ALANIS: Like you're coming back.

QUINN: We will.

ALANIS: Does pity have no bounds?

ARIANA: We will, Al. Whether you want us to or not.

ALANIS: Not.

ARIANA: Fine. Well, see ya.

QUINN: See ya.

ALANIS: Good riddance.

(QUINN and ARIANA exit.)

TALK BACK!

1. Are your parents involved in your extracurricular activities? Is this a good or a bad thing?

2. Do you think your parents are too critical or not interested enough or just right? Why?

3. Do you get excited or scared about performing in front of a crowd? Why?

4. How do you think you'd act in Alanis's situation?

5. Would you still want to be Alanis's friend? Why or why not?

6. If you could say one encouraging thing to Alanis, what would it be?

7. Do you think Ariana and Quinn will come back to visit Alanis again? Why or why not? Would you?

CHEAT

3F, 2M

WHO

FEMALES	MALES
Courtney	Chris
Giselle	JC
Julia	

WHERE Giselle's living room, suburbia.

WHEN Present day. Scene 2 takes place about ten minutes after Scene 1 ends.

☻ To act out something you may not have actually experienced in your life, try connecting to the character's feelings instead of the situation. For example, if you're supposed to play someone who's entire family died in a plane crash (but, hopefully, this hasn't happened to you), focus on a time when you felt sad or abandoned or alone, even if the exact circumstances surrounding your feelings were different.

☜ What would tear your world apart and make you rethink your life? Try thinking of a scenario where your trust was betrayed and write about it.

Scene 1: The Gift

JULIA: What are you doing tonight, Giselle?

GISELLE: I'm just hanging out at home.

CHRIS: Let's do something.

GISELLE: I can't.

JC: You never can.

GISELLE: Sure, I can.

COURTNEY: No, you never do.

GISELLE: Well, I'm having you guys over at my house right now. That's something, isn't it?

COURTNEY: Not really.

GISELLE: Sure it is!

JC: I was talking about going out places. You never go out places.

GISELLE: My parents don't like me to go out so much. They're protective.

CHRIS: Kinda overprotective. No offense.

GISELLE: Offense taken! They just care.

JULIA: Come on, Giselle, can't they make an exception sometime? We could go dancing!

CHRIS: I hate dancing.

JULIA: It doesn't have to be dancing. Just something.

GISELLE: It's a school night.

JC: So? Do your homework now.

GISELLE: I already did it.

COURTNEY: So what's the problem?

GISELLE: I just don't want to, OK?

JULIA: It's not your parents at all, is it? It's you who wants to stay in.

GISELLE: I want to stay in because my parents want me to and they care about me and I respect that. Is that so weird?

JC: A little.

GISELLE: No, really. Is it so strange to want to please your parents? I bet the rest of you want to all the time, too. Honestly, I have a hard time believing that all of you have no interest in making your parents proud. And not making them mad at you! I like it when my parents think I'm good and smart and no trouble. I'm not ashamed of that. Why am I supposed to pretend that I fight with my parents all the time when I don't? Where's the rulebook that says I'm supposed to hate them just because I'm a teenager? It's stupid. People just think their lives are supposed to be like people's on TV. People on TV have extra dramatic lives because otherwise TV would be boring! It's supposed to be more dramatic than real life or else no one would watch it! Excuse me for living, but I actually get along with and agree with my parents a lot. I think they're smart and nice. Not perfect, but really good parents for the most part.

CHRIS: That's the sickest thing I ever heard.

GISELLE: Shut up, Chris.

COURTNEY: So you really won't go out tonight?

JULIA: Don't we rate at all, Giselle? You spend almost every night with your parents. Would it be so terrible to do something with us for a change?

GISELLE: You know it's not that. I love you guys. Plus, I actually see more of you than I do of them, if you want to be mathematical about it. I see you all day long.

COURTNEY: Not really. In classes, we might be in the same room or building but we don't see each other.

GISELLE: Most of the time I'm home, I'm sleeping.

COURTNEY: I still think you see them more. What about the weekends?

(The doorbell rings.)

GISELLE: Hold on. I guess I should get that. If I don't come back in five seconds, call the police!

CHRIS: Man, your parents did raise you weird.

(GISELLE exits to answer the door.)

CHRIS: Was she serious?

JULIA: I think partly yes, partly no.

(Beat.)

JC: I got a new CD today. We could listen to that.

COURTNEY: What is it? Because I don't like that techno stuff you like.

(GISELLE reenters with a gift in her hand.)

JULIA: Ooo! Who's that for?

GISELLE: My mom.

JC: Is it her birthday?

GISELLE: No. It's not any occasion.

CHRIS: Who's it from?

COURTNEY: That's none of your business.

CHRIS: I was just asking a question.

GISELLE: I don't know.

JC: Is there a card?

GISELLE: Yes.

JC: Open it!

JULIA: That would be rude. It's not hers.

JC: Let me see!

(JC takes the gift from GISELLE's hands.)

GISELLE: Leave it alone, JC.

JC: The card envelope is not sealed!

GISELLE: It's probably from my dad.

COURTNEY: Your dad sends your mom gifts for no reason?

GISELLE: Well, no. Not usually.

JULIA: But he has before?

GISELLE: Well, no.

CHRIS: Maybe it's a bomb.

JC: No way. It's not ticking.

COURTNEY: You're curious, Giselle, aren't you?

GISELLE: Well, it's just unusual. That's all.

JC: If I open the card you can't get into trouble.

GISELLE: Don't open the card. It's not mine. Maybe it's a business thing or something.

CHRIS: Wouldn't they send that to work?

JC: Yeah.

GISELLE: I guess so.

JC: I could find out right now, Gis. Just say the word. Like I said, you couldn't get in trouble for it because I'm doing it.

CHRIS: If you really want to know . . .

COURTNEY: Do something unexpected for once. Something a teenager would do.

GISELLE: I *am* a teenager. I do teenager things all the time.

COURTNEY: No, you don't.

GISELLE: Sure, I do.

COURTNEY: No, you don't!

GISELLE: Definitionally, if I *am* a teenager, then it stands to reason that I do teenager things!

JC: Who's Larry?

GISELLE: I don't know—You opened it!

JC: Yeah.

(GISELLE grabs the card away from JC.)

GISELLE: You shouldn't have done that. I didn't give you permission to do that.

JC: Then maybe you should put it back in the envelope without looking at it.

CHRIS: You have to look at it now. It wouldn't make any sense, since the damage has already been done, to just put it back.

JC: No, just put it back.

(JULIA picks up on some weird vibes from JC.)

JULIA: Yeah, just put it back. No harm done.

GISELLE: You don't want me to look at it.

JC: Well . . .

JULIA: Maybe it's none of our business. Maybe it's a business thing like you said. What if you make your mom mad?

GISELLE: *(Reading.)* Dear Carol, I'm so crazy about you. When can you spend another night . . .

(Beat as GISELLE continues reading. CHRIS, COURTNEY, JULIA, and JC exchange worried glances.)

GISELLE: Oh my God.

JC: I bet it's a joke.

GISELLE: It's not a joke. It's real. *(Beat.)* **My whole life is a lie. This nice house, my nice family—it's all a joke! My mother is a lying, cheating . . . I can't believe it! And she lectures me day and night about** being honest, being good, not giving in to peer pressure, the dangers of . . . total hypocrite! I just don't know . . . I just can't believe this! And what am I supposed to do now? What am I supposed to do when my mom comes home? What can I say to her? I can't even look her in the face ever again. And my dad! What do I say to my dad? Am I supposed to pretend I don't know about this for the rest of my life? Am I supposed to just keep being the good little girl? Now that I know my whole, entire life is a lie? It's not possible! My poor Dad! I hate my mom. I hate her! I can't believe she did this to me! I can't believe she lied to me! I can't believe my whole family . . . How am I supposed to act? What am I supposed to do now?

JULIA: Maybe . . . maybe it is a joke. Maybe it's not how it seems.

GISELLE: Did you see this card? It's exactly how it seems. It says . . . too much!

CHRIS: Why do you think it got sent here?

GISELLE: To pull my family apart, that's why!

JC: I'm sorry, Giselle.

GISELLE: I hate you! I hate everyone! I have no family and I have no friends!

(GISELLE exits.)

Scene 2: The Fallout

(GISELLE reenters.)

GISELLE: Let's go out somewhere.

JULIA: I don't think that's a good idea.

GISELLE: You're not the boss of me. I can do whatever I want.

JULIA: I know.

COURTNEY: You don't have to be mad at us. We didn't do anything wrong.

(A tense beat as GISELLE stares at COURTNEY.)

GISELLE: I know. Sorry.

JC: You don't have to be sorry.

CHRIS: It's . . . It sucks, what's going on with . . . You know what I mean.

GISELLE: I just can't believe . . . my mom! Who is always perfect . . . with another man! It's wrong. It's so, so wrong!

JULIA: We know, Giselle.

(Beat.)

GISELLE: Who wants a drink?

JULIA: What?

GISELLE: I'm opening the liquor cabinet. Who wants something? As I see it, we can drink everything in it and do whatever we want. I deserve it. I have a lot of living to make up for. I've been good for too long. Listening all my life to a bunch of lies about being a good girl, doing what you're told. Not any more. I'm doing whatever I want, whenever I want. It makes sense to start with getting drunk. Isn't that what they do on TV? I'm now going to be a TV teen—smoking, drinking, having abortions—whatever! Anything goes! Apparently, that's how the world is. Even my perfect mother is a huge whore, so why shouldn't I be? Life starts today, boys. So let's not waste any more time. *(Looking through the liquor cabinet.)* Who wants whiskey? What's the worst thing I can drink here? Oh, does anyone have drugs? Let's not waste any time. I think that's the next step after drunkenness. No time to waste, people! Stop staring at me, and someone find a way to make me a TV teen already! I need to get really messed up before my parents get home.

CHRIS: Uh, Giselle? You're sort of losing it.

GISELLE: Exactly. That's the point, stupid.

JULIA: Let's not rush into anything. You're mad at your mom. You shouldn't destroy yourself. Besides, I hate to say it, but all the things your mom said to you before about being good and honest and all that, it was right. I know what she did, having an affair, is wrong, but it doesn't make what she taught you wrong. It just means she was wrong for not following her own advice. Right?

GISELLE: Wrong. It's all crap.

JULIA: No, seriously. Maybe it's hard to hear this, but your mom is still right about all that other stuff. Maybe . . . I don't know . . .

GISELLE: No, you don't know!

JULIA: Maybe she just wants your life to be better than hers.

COURTNEY: It's possible. It's a very parent thing to want you to be more perfect than they are.

CHRIS: And to try to seem perfect themselves. I mean, they're human, too—

GISELLE: But they're not supposed to be. They're supposed to be better than this. They're supposed to know better and *do* better. They're supposed to be *adults*. And *married*. And they're not supposed to screw up their whole family like this.

JULIA: All this—what your mom did—is definitely not good, but it doesn't make all the other stuff bad, does it? Don't answer that, think about it! Your mom still loves you even if she did something stupid. So don't screw up who you are and your whole life just because of what she did. You're not the girl on TV who gets pregnant at fourteen, Giselle. That's not who you are.

GISELLE: I could be. Maybe I should be. You were just saying a little while ago that I was boring. That I never do anything fun. Well, I'm going to start being fun! How do you make a martini? What is a martini, anyway? Anybody know anything about this stuff or should I just experiment?

(Beat.)

COURTNEY: You're freaking me out. Seriously, you're acting really weird.

GISELLE: Good!

(GISELLE takes a bunch of bottles out and starts pouring a little bit from each bottle into a glass.)

CHRIS: I don't think that's a good idea.

GISELLE: I didn't ask you what you think.

JC: That'll make you sick.

GISELLE: Perfect. I'll act on the outside how I feel on the inside. Like puking. Disgusted.

COURTNEY: You've totally lost it. Come back to earth, Giselle.

GISELLE: I hate my mother.

COURTNEY: Welcome to the real world. A lot of people do.

GISELLE: Do you?

COURTNEY: Not hate exactly. It depends on the day. Some days yes, some days no.

GISELLE: Is your mother a lying whore?

COURTNEY: Not that I know of.

GISELLE: Well, then. I guess I should hate mine more.

JC: Maybe you shouldn't say things like that.

GISELLE: Why not?

JC: I don't know. What if she died today and these were your last words?

GISELLE: Good riddance.

JC: You don't mean that.

GISELLE: Maybe I do.

JULIA: You don't.

CHRIS: Don't say things you'll regret.

COURTNEY: Maybe we should work on what you should say to your mom.

GISELLE: I'm not speaking to her ever again.

COURTNEY: You don't want to tell her how you feel?

GISELLE: I'll tell her off, then I'll never speak to her again.

CHRIS: What about your dad?

GISELLE: My parents will split up and I'll live with my dad.

JC: Most kids live with the mom.

GISELLE: I would die first. I don't want to live with her.

CHRIS: You might have to.

GISELLE: I'll run away.

COURTNEY: To where?

GISELLE: Who cares?

CHRIS: But you won't be able to see your dad either, then.

JULIA: I think we've gone too far with all this. Let's step back for a sec. First of all, do you definitely want to say something to your mom about this?

GISELLE: I think I have to. I don't think I could keep this a secret. I'm so mad!

JULIA: OK.

CHRIS: What if your dad comes home first?

JC: Oh my God. That would be bad. Or if you can't talk to your mom alone.

GISELLE: Should I tell my dad? I don't know. I don't want to. I mean, I do, but I don't. I want her to tell him. Or maybe not. Maybe I . . . I don't want my family broken up. I want them to stay together. I know I hate my mom, but still . . . And I don't want her to break my dad's heart. I don't know . . .

COURTNEY: Make her decide.

CHRIS: Decide what?

COURTNEY: Whether to tell your dad. Just tell her you know.

GISELLE: But then she'll know I saw the card!

COURTNEY: Tell her JC opened it. It's the truth.

JC: Oh great. I never thought—

COURTNEY: Shut up, JC. You do the crime, you do the time. Just tell her you saw the card and let her deal with the rest. She's supposed to be the adult, right? Let her clean up her own mess. That's not your job.

GISELLE: I don't know how I'm ever going to look at her again.

CHRIS: I hear a car door!

JULIA: Who is it?

(CHRIS goes over to a window.)

CHRIS: Your mom, Giselle.

JC: I guess this is it . . .

TALK BACK!

1. How would you handle a situation like Giselle's?

2. Does one mistake (like Giselle's mother's affair) cancel out any other good things in a person's life?

3. Have you ever felt betrayed? When and why?

4. Do you try to please your parents? How?

5. Are your parents' expectations for you higher than their expectations for themselves? Is that fair or unfair?

6. Why do teens rebel against their parents? What's the goal?

REVOLUTION

3F, 4M

WHO

FEMALES	MALES
Annette	Jacques
Marie	Jean-Paul
Michelle	Pierre
	Robbie

WHERE A room in a large French chateau just outside Paris.

WHEN 1789.

🎭 Think about status. How might rich and poor people move differently? How might they talk differently? Also, remember this is literally a life or death situation for all the characters!

✍ Write an ending for this play.

Scene 1: Fight or Flee

JACQUES: It's begun.

MARIE: No, it couldn't be.

JEAN-PAUL: Jacques is right. We heard it from the maid.

MARIE: What are we to do?

ANNETTE: I'm frightened. Are they really going to chop our heads off?

JACQUES: I don't know.

JEAN-PAUL: We won't let them.

MARIE: But is that *really* what's happening? I can't believe that's really happening. It's too horrible.

ANNETTE: What did we ever do to deserve anything like that?

JEAN-PAUL: We're rich.

MARIE: We can hardly help it. We were born into it. It's not like we can do anything about it.

JACQUES: I don't think it matters.

JEAN-PAUL: They were born into being poor and suffering. They see all we have and . . .

ANNETTE: They want to kill us? It's not fair!

JEAN-PAUL: Life isn't fair.

MARIE: I hate it when people say that! Life *should* be fair! We should expect it to be fair. Isn't that sort of what fair means? That what ought to happen, happens? Why should I accept less? Why should anyone? It's not fair that people are poor and starving, but it's also not fair that we should be punished for our good fortune. Let's face it: until you're an adult, you don't really have power over your life. You live the life you're born into, the life your parents made for you. We happen to be born of wealthy parents who are part of the nobility. The same was true of peasants' parents. It makes us lucky, but it doesn't make us evil. Right now, we are victims of our birth as much as the poor are. What are we to do? We're powerless. Are we meant to just sit here and wait for them to come and kill us? It's too terrible. I can't die! I don't want to die. I'm young! I have a lot to do still. I can't believe people are so horrible. And I refuse to accept that life is unfair. I will make it fair. Let's fight them.

JACQUES: That doesn't make sense. How will you make life fair? And we can't fight them. There are too many of them. We are only four children.

MARIE: Well, I won't accept what's unfair! I won't wait for the ax to fall on my head!

JEAN-PAUL: They are coming now. I can hear them. We don't have any time to waste.

ANNETTE: Shall we hide?

JACQUES: Or run?

MARIE: Or fight?

JEAN-PAUL: They'll find us if we hide. They'll catch us if we run. They'll kill us if we fight.

ANNETTE: Then what are we to do? We're trapped up here!

JACQUES: We could pretend to be poor! To be one of them!

MARIE: These clothes will give us away, Jacques! No one would believe us.

JACQUES: We could get other clothes. From the servants.

MARIE: How do we know the servants don't want us dead, too? If the mob is inside, someone had to let them in. Maybe they want us dead, too! Oh God, what are we to do?

JEAN-PAUL: Stay calm. Marie is right; we look too much like rich children. And they will stop at nothing to find us. We have no choice but to try to get out of the house undetected. We don't know if the servants in the house are against us.

ANNETTE: I always thought they loved us.

JEAN-PAUL: We have not always behaved well around them. Just last week you threw a fit, Annette, that gave one of the maids a black eye.

ANNETTE: I wanted to wear my pink dress and I wanted lemon cake.

JEAN-PAUL: We will have to say good-bye to this life once we leave, you realize. No fancy dresses and cakes. But at least we will have a life. We will be poor. We will live on the streets. And no one must ever, ever know about our present lives. You can never brag to anyone about who you were or what you had. We are going to be peasants now. Any slip-ups and we are dead. Do you understand?

(JACQUES, MARIE, and ANNETTE nod in agreement.)

ANNETTE: Can I take any of my things?

JEAN-PAUL: No. We must take nothing. Remember, we are street urchins. We are poor.

ANNETTE: What if I said I stole it from a rich girl?

JACQUES: Do you want to have your head chopped off?

MARIE: Hurry, Jean-Paul! What should we do? I hear them shouting!

JEAN-PAUL: We must . . .

MARIE: Hurry!

JEAN-PAUL: I don't know!

JACQUES: We need to think of something!

JEAN-PAUL: But there's no way out that doesn't involve jumping from a high window.

ANNETTE: Maybe it would be better than getting your head chopped off.

JACQUES: Well, I for one want to get out alive and unhurt.

JEAN-PAUL: No matter what, we must stick together. If we get out of here, we must help each other survive and we must never, never reveal our true identities. Agreed?

MARIE: Yes! Of course!

JEAN-PAUL: Annette?

ANNETTE: I won't tell.

JACQUES: Not even to brag?

ANNETTE: I don't brag!

JACQUES: You do!

JEAN-PAUL: Annette?

ANNETTE: Yes!

JEAN-PAUL: I think our best bet is to disguise ourselves as Jacques suggested. We must start pretending now that we're poor. We must blend into the mob. Mess up your hair. Get your plainest clothes—wrap in sheets from the beds! It may not work, but we've got to get out of here.

MARIE: I hear them right outside!

JEAN-PAUL: Wait for a bit, then pretend you're looting.

JACQUES: Do you think they're stealing our stuff? That's not fair. If anyone touches my—

MARIE: Shut up, Jacques! Of course they're taking your things.

JEAN-PAUL: Make yourself look as disheveled as possible!

MARIE: Come on, Annette! This is life or death!

(The door slams open. MICHELLE, PIERRE, and LUC enter.)

JEAN-PAUL: Close the door!

(LUC closes the door.)

MARIE: There are such nice things in here!

PIERRE: How long have you been here?

JACQUES: Not long.

LUC: Long enough to get dressed in their clothes.

JEAN-PAUL: Right.

ANNETTE: They're pretty.

MICHELLE: How did you get here before us? We thought we were the first.

LUC: We've been very fast.

PIERRE: The fastest of anyone, I would say.

MARIE: We—

JEAN-PAUL: We came right to the top. We thought we'd work from the bottom down.

MICHELLE: Weren't you worried you'd be caught if they set the place on fire?

JACQUES: We're not afraid of anything!

LUC: Not even getting your heads chopped off?

ANNETTE: I'm scared of that.

JACQUES: Shut up, Annette.

PIERRE: Annette? Isn't one of the daughters of the house named Annette?

ANNETTE: I like that name. So I took it.

MICHELLE: You're very clean.

ANNETTE: I like to be clean.

JEAN-PAUL: We bathed in the river this morning.

PIERRE: Are you related?

JACQUES: Are you?

PIERRE: Yes.

JACQUES: So are we.

JEAN-PAUL: We think. Never knew our mother.

MICHELLE: Neither did we. Except Luc. He remembers her before she died.

ANNETTE: Your mother died?

LUC: Yes. So what?

PIERRE: What happened to your mother if she didn't die?

JEAN-PAUL: She . . . run off.

MARIE: She *ran* off.

LUC: Oh, excuse you. Aren't you proper?

MARIE: Well, no—

JEAN-PAUL: *(To MARIE.)* See? You're a pain, Nina. I'm always telling her that. She thinks if she puts on a rich girl's dress, she can put on her manners, too.

PIERRE: Better watch out no one decides to guillotine you for your good manners.

JACQUES: Are they really chopping heads off?

LUC: Ain't you seen it?

JACQUES: Well, yes. Of course we . . . has.

JEAN-PAUL: *(To JACQUES.)* Don't lie, Richard. We ain't seen a thing. Been too busy looting.

MICHELLE: Looks like you done well for yourselves.

PIERRE: We thought we was the best.

LUC: We *are* the best. I can't believe you got up here before us. I've never seen you before. I think you're fakes. I think you're the rich kids of this house.

(Beat.)

JEAN-PAUL: Can you keep a secret?

Scene 2: Live or Die

MICHELLE: Of course we can. We haven't survived this long by blabbing everything we know.

JEAN-PAUL: Fine. I'll tell you our secret.

MARIE: Can we trust them? It could mean our deaths if they tell!

JEAN-PAUL: Can we trust you?

LUC: We haven't turned you in yet.

(Beat.)

JEAN-PAUL: Our secret is . . . we're thieves.

LUC: Ah. Can *you* keep a secret?

MARIE: Yes!

LUC: So are we.

PIERRE: Everyone's a thief these days. Or we'd all die of starvation.

JACQUES: Yes, but we're *big* thieves!

JEAN-PAUL: Quiet, Richard. We mustn't say any more.

MICHELLE: Why?

JEAN-PAUL: It could be dangerous.

MICHELLE: Why?

ANNETTE: Yeah, why?

(*JEAN-PAUL is mysteriously silent.*)

LUC: I think you're a liar. I think you're a member of royalty trying to save your neck. I think we could get a nice reward for turning you in.

PIERRE: Plus we could watch your heads bounce as they chop them off of your necks.

JEAN-PAUL: My brother here is right. We are big thieves. We take expensive items. Jewels.

ANNETTE: Dresses!

LUC: Oh yeah? What do you do with them afterward?

JACQUES: Sell them!

PIERRE: Where?

MARIE: The market!

MICHELLE: You can't sell things like that in the market. You'd get robbed blind.

LUC: No one brings gobs of money to the market. You'd have to go on the black market if you was to make a proper profit.

ANNETTE: That's where we go. A different market. A black market. Everything is black there.

JACQUES: Shut up, Annette!

ANNETTE: You shut up, Jacques!

LUC: I thought he was named Richard.

PIERRE: I knew you was liars! You *is* royalty trash. And you're going to die. I say we turn them in.

MICHELLE: I say we take their things, then turn them in.

LUC: I say we watch them beg pathetically for their lives, take their things, then turn them in.

JEAN-PAUL: No! Not them. Just me. Turn me in if you want. I'm the oldest. You don't need to see all of us die. My brother and sisters are very clever, and loyal. Help them get free, and they can help you steal or do whatever you need to do to survive.

MICHELLE: Please. They'd be more mouths to feed. And they'd be helpless on the streets. We'd have to care for them like babies. They'd die anyway.

JEAN-PAUL: Maybe we do know very little of your ways and what you need to do to survive. We live lives of luxury. I admit it. We do feel safe, my brother and sisters and I, most of the time—except for today, of course. But it's not our fault we were born into this life, this family. We can't very well help being royalty any more than you can help being a peasant. It's not your fault that you need to steal to eat, and it's not our fault that we only need to ring a bell to get a meal. We have no control over what our parents do or the family we're born into. Actually, we hardly ever see our parents. We're as alone as you are. Our parents may as well be dead.

PIERRE: They will be soon.

MARIE: This is so terrible!

JEAN-PAUL: Please. If you must get your reward and you wish to see blood, make it mine. Let them go free.

ANNETTE: No, Jean-Paul! It was my fault we were caught. I should die.

JEAN-PAUL: Don't worry, Annette. You didn't mean to give us away. I'll take care of things.

LUC: Don't argue. You might all die yet.

MARIE: You can't mean this! You can't want us to die.

PIERRE: Why not? We spend every day having nothing and you have everything. Why shouldn't we want you to die?

ANNETTE: Because it's wrong to want people to die!

LUC: People die on the street of starvation all the time.

JACQUES: That's not the same.

MICHELLE: Sure it is! Do you know who's killing us?

ANNETTE: Who?

MICHELLE: You! The rich! Royalty! You have more than you could ever need while we have nothing at all. You give nothing and you take everything!

JEAN-PAUL: Can't you get jobs?

LUC: Waiting on you?

ANNETTE: Yes! We could get you hired as a maid and stable boys. Do you like horses—

JEAN-PAUL: Quiet, Annette! I'm sure you wouldn't want to work here, but there are other jobs you could do, aren't there?

PIERRE: Like what?

MARIE: Shops! You could work in shops.

MICHELLE: And we could pay such high taxes to you that we have no money left for ourselves!

JACQUES: That's not true!

LUC: How would you know?

JACQUES: Because it's not! It's not our fault. You don't pay me. I don't eat your food.

MICHELLE: It is true. All of it!

JEAN-PAUL: Then teach us. Show us! We could be valuable to you, too. You can take all we have now.

PIERRE: We was going to do that anyway.

JEAN-PAUL: But we could give you more. We know other people's houses. Where they keep their valuables. We have a lot of information that could be helpful to you.

MARIE: Jean-Paul, I don't know if this is right!

JEAN-PAUL: Would you rather die?

MARIE: No.

PIERRE: What do you think, Luc? Are they telling the truth? Can they be trusted? Or are they just desperate to live?

LUC: Both, I think. Desperate and honest.

PIERRE: But which would be better, having them live or die?

MICHELLE: Do you really think we could even get them out of here?

LUC: We could, if we wanted to.

MICHELLE: They'd be four more mouths to feed on the streets.

PIERRE: But if they really know where we can find jewels and things . . .

(MARIE gets up and opens a drawer, pulling out a necklace.)

MARIE: Here. You can have this. It's my favorite. I think it's valuable.

(PIERRE grabs the necklace.)

PIERRE: You *think* it's valuable? Are these diamonds?

MARIE: Yes.

PIERRE: I've never seen diamonds up close. Do you think they're for real?

ANNETTE: Of course they're real! What else would they be?

PIERRE: Paste.

ANNETTE: How can you make a necklace out of paste?

JACQUES: They can make fake ones. In fact . . .

LUC: What?

JACQUES: I don't know if I should say . . .

(JACQUES looks nervously at JEAN-PAUL.)

JEAN-PAUL: Go ahead. Tell them.

JACQUES: Well, our mother—

MARIE: Wait! We should get a promise. If we are going to reveal everything, we should know that we will live. If we are going to die, I don't think we should give these urchins everything we have!

LUC: We could have you killed if you don't tell.

MARIE: You could have us killed if we do tell.

ANNETTE: Don't tell, Jacques!

PIERRE: Very well. I'll call in the mob. They might not

even get you to the guillotine to have your head chopped off. They might decide to tear you limb from limb right here and now.

JEAN-PAUL: We are at an impasse. You want the riches we can give you, don't you?

MICHELLE: Yes.

JEAN-PAUL: And we want to live. We want to escape this place. Can't we work together? Can't we come up with an arrangement that works for all of us?

LUC: Keep talking.

JEAN-PAUL: We know where our mother hides her real jewels. What the others will find will be fakes. She's had each piece of jewelry copied. The location of the originals is known only by my mother, her loyal maid who will not tell, and us.

ANNETTE: I don't know where they are.

JEAN-PAUL: I know the location of jewels the size of your fist. My sister's necklace is nothing in comparison. Necklaces of red rubies, ropes of sapphires, sparkling diamond tiaras, rings of every shape and color, earrings so heavy you can't lift your chin—all this could be yours. But only if you get us out of here, safe and alive. All of us.

PIERRE: Don't want to be a martyr anymore?

JEAN-PAUL: I don't want to die any more than you do. I may be pampered, I may not know much about how to be poor and live on the streets, but my will to live is as strong as yours. I can and will survive on my wits, given the chance.

LUC: I think you might.

JEAN-PAUL: If we can get some other clothes, we can blend into the crowd, get the jewels, and get out with no one being the wiser.

MICHELLE: The servant's quarters are just above us. We could take their clothes.

PIERRE: I don't know . . .

JACQUES: Please. We could make you rich!

ANNETTE: Please. We're just kids, like you!

MARIE: Please. Have a heart.

PIERRE: I don't know. Luc?

MICHELLE: I think they're telling the truth.

LUC: I don't know . . .

JEAN-PAUL: You have our lives in your hands. And we have the power to give you everything you've ever wanted.

LUC: So you say.

PIERRE: What do you think, Luc?

TALK BACK!

1. What do you think happens in the end?

2. Is it fair for the poor to take from the rich?

3. Is it OK to use violence to get what you want, even if the result is good? For example, during the French Revolution royalty were killed so that France could be more fair and democratic.

4. Why was the guillotine used to kill people during the French Revolution?

5. Children as well as adults were killed during the French Revolution. Is it more unfair to kill children under these circumstances than adults?

6. Can you understand why the peasants wanted to see the rich die?

7. Huge crowds used to gather to see public executions. What draws people to watch violence?

AFTERMATH

1F, 4M

WHO

FEMALES	MALES
Marnie	Ari
	Leo
	Sam
	Tim

WHERE Scene 1: Sam and Tim's house; Scene 2: Outside.

WHEN Present day.

🎭 In this play, it's important to *think* like your character and go beyond just saying your lines. For example, there's a lot that goes through Sam's mind that he doesn't say. When he hesitates, what is he thinking?

✍ This play is about the people you don't hear about in news stories. Write a play about the long-term effects of a crime. You can view it from the victim's, the witness's, or the criminal's point of view.

Scene 1: See

SAM: Mom?

TIM: Just me.

SAM: When are Mom or Dad going to be home?

TIM: Dunno.

SAM: Oh.

TIM: You OK?

SAM: Sure. Yeah.

TIM: You look confused.

SAM: No.

TIM: OK.

(Beat.)

TIM: There's one more piece of pizza left from last night in the fridge.

SAM: OK.

(SAM stands still.)

TIM: You're sure acting weird.

SAM: Can I tell you something, Tim?

TIM: Sure.

SAM: I saw a dead body today.

TIM: Did somebody die?

SAM: I guess so.

TIM: What do you mean you guess so?

SAM: I mean the person was dead. I didn't see them die or anything, though.

TIM: Then how do you know they were dead?

SAM: I could tell, OK?

TIM: How?

SAM: She just looked dead, OK?

TIM: She?

SAM: Yeah.

TIM: Where did you see her?

SAM: In the woods.

TIM: Was anyone with you?

SAM: No.

(Beat.)

SAM: She wasn't moving. And . . . she looked like she'd been there for a while.

TIM: Was she old?

SAM: No.

TIM: Young?

SAM: I don't want to talk about it.

TIM: You brought it up.

   (Beat.)

SAM: Young, OK? She was young. Young-ish.

TIM: Was she killed, you think? Murdered or something?

SAM: I think . . . I think yes. I think so.

TIM: Was she all gory?

SAM: Let's just . . . Shut up, Tim. Never mind.

TIM: You keep saying that, then you keep talking anyway.

SAM: Well, it's just that . . . I don't know. It was bad. I
   could tell. It wasn't so much that she was all bloody
   or anything. But . . . you could just tell. It wasn't right.

TIM: Did you tell the police?

SAM: I didn't know . . . I wasn't sure . . . Not yet.

TIM: You'd better tell them.

SAM: There were bugs on her.

TIM: She was there for a while then.

SAM: That's what I said.

(Beat.)

SAM: I never saw anybody dead before. At least not dead like that. I saw Uncle Dave. And people on TV, I think. But never so close. And never anybody who wasn't old. And never anyone . . . Tim, it was so creepy how her skin looked and that there were bugs crawling on her. It didn't seem right. She was so white. And it was . . . it was such a sunny day outside. That's why I went walking in the first place. It was such a nice day. So I went out to the woods by myself. I was thinking of how the sun looked coming through the trees like . . . Well, it always looks like a scene from a movie where God or an angel or something comes to announce some-thing to someone. Sounds dumb I guess. But that's what I was thinking, and then there she was. Right there in the sun. And she had a shirt on with Oscar the Grouch on it. It seemed so weird. She had a kids' shirt on. *(Beat.)* I don't want to go back out there, Tim. The police are going to make me go back out there.

TIM: You have to.

SAM: But I don't want to.

TIM: Yeah, but someone's wondering where she is.

SAM: If they were wondering, why didn't they find her? She wasn't hard to find.

TIM: They don't know where to look.

SAM: If I tell the police, maybe they'll just look for themselves. I can just tell them sort of where it is. I don't even know that I could find her again, actually. I wasn't really looking where I was going. Maybe I can't even find her again.

TIM: You said she was easy to find.

SAM: Well . . . Maybe it's weird, but I'm not going back there.

TIM: You have to. Someone wants to find her. Someone's wondering where she is. And you know. And maybe someone killed that girl. That person could be on the loose. You have to tell the police you found her. And, if they want you to, you have to show them, Sam. You have to. If you were dead, wouldn't you want someone to tell Mom and Dad?

SAM: No. I wouldn't want them to see me like that.

TIM: Yes, you would. You wouldn't care what you looked like anymore. You'd be dead. And they'd want to know where you were. They'd want justice, too. Besides, you'll be sort of a hero. I bet the parents will be grateful, like I said. You'd get on the news.

SAM: I don't want to be on the news.

TIM: What are you so scared of? She's dead. She's not going to get you.

SAM: I know.

TIM: You could get put in jail if they find out you knew where a dead girl was but didn't say anything.

SAM: Only if someone tells them.

TIM: I'll tell them if you don't.

SAM: You wouldn't!

TIM: I would. You have to tell, Sam. You just have to. It's just the right thing to do. If you weren't such a chicken, you'd see that for yourself.

SAM: Maybe the killer is still around, Tim! Ever think of that?

TIM: You don't know for sure she was killed.

SAM: Why else would she be in the middle of the woods?

TIM: Maybe she fell. Or maybe she got lost and starved to death.

SAM: She didn't starve to death.

TIM: How do you know?

SAM: I know.

TIM: How?

SAM: She wasn't super skinny, OK?

TIM: Maybe she killed herself.

(Beat.)

SAM: I don't think so.

TIM: How do you know, Sam? You just don't know. That's why there are police investigations.

SAM: She was killed, OK? I know it.

TIM: How?

SAM: Her—she—her shirt. Her shirt. I don't want to talk about it, Tim.

TIM: The police are going to ask. You may as well get used to it. They might ask you over and over again. They might think you killed her.

SAM: I didn't kill her! I wouldn't!

TIM: I know. But I'm just trying to prepare you.

SAM: I couldn't do that.

TIM: So you'd better get used to telling the facts and not getting all upset or they'll think you did it.

SAM: I didn't do it. I'm just a kid.

TIM: Kids kill people.

SAM: Not me. Besides . . . Whoever killed her was sick. I'm not like that.

TIM: There's more to this, isn't there?

SAM: I don't want to talk about it.

TIM: I'm calling the police.

SAM: Come on, Tim, don't!

TIM: I have to. You have to tell what you saw, Sam.

Scene 2: Touch

(MARNIE crosses the stage.)

ARI: Look! There's the girl whose sister died.

LEO: She looks sad.

ARI: Her sister died. Wouldn't you look sad?

LEO: No.

ARI: If she *died* you would.

LEO: Well, maybe if she actually died.

SAM: Don't stare at her.

LEO: Why not?

ARI: Everybody's staring.

LEO: She's probably used to it. She's on the news every night.

ARI: Did they ever find the guy?

SAM: No.

ARI: You never hear the end of news stories, seems like. You always hear the beginning but not the end.

LEO: I heard she was naked.

ARI: Who?

LEO: The girl, when they found her.

SAM: She wasn't.

LEO: That would have been cool.

ARI: It would be excellent to find a dead body, wouldn't it?

LEO: Must be creepy.

ARI: But really cool. Have you ever touched a dead person?

LEO: My mom made me kiss my grandma after she died. She was in a coffin!

ARI: Gross! Dead grandma skin!

LEO: Don't remind me!

ARI: Why did you do it?

LEO: I was little. I thought I had to.

ARI: Oh, man, that is gross!

LEO: I know!

ARI: How about you, Sam?

SAM: No.

ARI: Me neither. I've never even seen one.

LEO: Never? How about your grandparents?

ARI: They're all alive.

LEO: How about your grandparents, Sam?

SAM: Still alive.

LEO: I'm the only one who saw a dead body?

ARI: I guess so. Hey! So are you two coming to my house to play Quest?

SAM: My mom said I have to go home and do my homework tonight.

LEO: Your mom is being really strict lately. You're like a prisoner.

SAM: Well, I'm not doing so well in classes, I guess.

ARI: Well, quit it already. It's getting boring.

SAM: Right.

LEO: Let's go.

ARI: Later.

> (ARI and LEO exit. SAM sits down by himself and looks off into the distance. After a beat, he stands up again. MARNIE enters. SAM sees her.)

MARNIE: Hi.

SAM: Hi.

MARNIE: What are you doing here?

SAM: Nothing. What are you doing here?

MARNIE: Nothing. I just . . .

SAM: What?

MARNIE: I just heard . . . did you find my sister?

SAM: Oh. Yeah.

MARNIE: You never said anything.

SAM: I don't exactly know you.

MARNIE: Well, you do now. I mean, you must know who I am.

SAM: What was I supposed to do? Introduce myself as the guy that found your dead sister?

MARNIE: That not what I meant!

SAM: Sorry. I didn't mean to say it like that.

MARNIE: But you did.

SAM: Sorry. Really. I didn't mean to . . .

MARNIE: I know. So . . . You're Sam.

SAM: Right.

MARNIE: I'm Marnie.

SAM: I know.

MARNIE: Right. So . . . It was here.

SAM: What?

MARNIE: Where you found her.

SAM: Not here.

MARNIE: Well, up ahead.

SAM: Yeah.

MARNIE: I would think that you wouldn't want to come here.

SAM: I don't. I didn't.

MARNIE: But you do now?

SAM: Well, yes and no.

MARNIE: Yes and no?

SAM: I don't *want* to come. I just find myself here. I guess that doesn't make sense to you.

MARNIE: No, it does. I'm here.

SAM: Yeah. How come you're here?

MARNIE: Same reason. Don't want to, but do want to at the same time. I couldn't come anywhere near here for a long time.

SAM: Me, too.

MARNIE: Sam? Will you show me?

SAM: Show you what?

MARNIE: Where you found her.

SAM: No!

MARNIE: Come on, Sam. She was my sister.

SAM: So? I'm still not going.

MARNIE: Then why are you here?

SAM: I don't know.

MARNIE: Please, Sam.

SAM: Why should I?

MARNIE: Because I want to know. She was my sister!

SAM: So what? No one even thinks about me. No one even knows about me. I didn't want them to, but now . . . I don't get why this is supposed to just disappear. I'm just supposed to forget. I can't forget. And I can't help you. I don't want to. I don't care if that's selfish. I don't get why I'm not allowed to be selfish. You got to take time off of school. You get everyone feeling sorry for you. No one feels sorry for me. No one thinks about what I saw. It was horrible, OK? I saw a dead person, and not an old one. And she looked . . . Is that what you want to know? Do you want to know what she looked like? 'Cause I don't think you do. You don't want to know any more than I want to know. And you're not allowed to tell me what to do. I don't care if your sister died. You're still not allowed to tell me what to do whenever you want. So just leave me alone.

MARNIE: I don't . . . Do you think I like being "the sister of the dead girl"? I don't. I hate it. I'd rather have my sister alive, believe it or not, than have everyone feeling sorry for me. And I don't feel sorry for you. Not at all. Not a bit. No one you know died. No one you were related to and mattered. No one you know was murdered. Do you know I'm scared all the time now? Do you know that I'm worried that he'll come back for me? And I go into my sister's room by accident sometimes because I forget. And I'm invisible to my parents. All they can think about is Emma. It's like I don't exist. And you think I'm supposed to feel sorry for you? You think we're the same? We're not the same. You're just mean. And selfish. So don't worry about that. You're selfish whether you're allowed to be or not. Forget I ever asked.

SAM: Listen, I'm sorry. But can't you understand what I'm saying? You don't want to know. *I* don't want to know. I wish I could forget. I wish it more than anything. Trust me, you don't want to know any more. I close my eyes every night and see your sister. You should remember her alive. You shouldn't see her dead.

MARNIE: So you won't show me?

SAM: You don't want to know.

MARNIE: You're a creep.

(MARNIE exits.)

TALK BACK!

1. What would you do if you saw evidence of a crime?

2. Can you understand why Sam wouldn't want to tell anyone what he saw? Why or why not?

3. Why do you think Sam and Marnie go back to the crime scene?

4. What would you suggest to Sam to help him cope with what he's seen?

5. If you were Marnie, would you want to know more about what happened to your sister? Why or why not?

6. How do you think you'd treat Marnie? Could you act normally or would you need to treat her differently if you knew her story?

7. Is Marnie being unfair to Sam or is Sam being unfair to Marnie?

CONCERTED EFFORT

4M

WHO
    MALES
        Harris
        Jeff
        Liam
        Teddy

WHERE Scene 1: Outside school; Scene 2: Outside a stadium.

WHEN Present day.

What are the dynamics between these characters? Who's the most powerful person in the group? Whom does your character respect and whom doesn't he respect?

Use three people you know and yourself as characters. Put the four of you in a situation where you *have* to interact and solve a problem. See who ends up being a leader, who gets his or her way, who crumbles under the pressure, etc.

Scene 1: Forbidden

LIAM: I can't.

TEDDY: What do you mean, you can't?

LIAM: What do you mean, what do I mean I can't?

TEDDY: What?

HARRIS: Why can't you?

LIAM: My parents won't let me.

HARRIS: Why?

LIAM: Because they think I'm going to take drugs and drink and get killed and be robbed. I don't know. Because they're stupid.

JEFF: But you have to go.

LIAM: I know!

HARRIS: Didn't you tell them?

LIAM: I did. They don't listen.

JEFF: Did you say it was important?

LIAM: Yes.

TEDDY: They won't let you go?

LIAM: I did! I tried everything.

JEFF: So are you going?

LIAM: Didn't you hear me? My parents won't let me go.

JEFF: So are you going?

LIAM: What do you mean?

HARRIS: Yeah. Jeff is right, Liam.

LIAM: Right about what?

HARRIS: You should go anyway.

LIAM : How?

JEFF: Just go. We'll make up a story.

LIAM: My parents would kill me if they found out.

JEFF: How would they find out?

LIAM: I don't know.

JEFF: Will you tell them, Harris?

HARRIS: No.

JEFF: How about you, Teddy? Will you tell Liam's parents?

TEDDY: No. Unless they tortured me for the information. Then I might.

HARRIS: They won't torture you, dummy.

TEDDY: Then no.

JEFF: So, are you going?

LIAM: Well . . .

HARRIS: They're not going to find out.

LIAM: It just seems like they might.

JEFF: How?

LIAM: I don't know how.

TEDDY: Parents have ways.

LIAM: I might feel guilty. Or mess up and forget the lie I told them!

TEDDY: Yeah, what if he messed up?

JEFF: Listen, your dad is going to drive us there and pick us up, right, Teddy?

TEDDY: Right.

HARRIS: Did you mention that to your parents, Liam?

LIAM: Well, I told them that Teddy's dad was driving us.

JEFF: What if he went with us? Then could you go?

LIAM: I don't know. Maybe.

JEFF: So tell them that.

HARRIS: Yeah!

TEDDY: But my dad isn't going to come.

JEFF: He wouldn't have to come. Liam just needs to say your dad's *going* to come.

LIAM: But what if they talk to Teddy's dad?

JEFF: Why would they?

LIAM: They could.

JEFF: Fine. If you don't want to go, don't go.

LIAM: I do want to go.

HARRIS: So you have to think of a way.

JEFF: He doesn't want to go.

TEDDY: I thought you wanted to go! I got you a ticket!

LIAM: I *do* want to go. I completely want to go.

HARRIS: So? Do what you have to do to go.

TEDDY: It's going to be a good time. And if you don't go, I need the money for the ticket anyway, 'cause you said you'd go.

LIAM: I want to go! I've been waiting my whole life to go! I liked their music before anyone else. I want to go more than any of you.

JEFF: So stop being a baby and go.

LIAM: You make it seem so simple.

HARRIS: If you really wanted to go, you'd think of a way.

LIAM: You guys, I really, really want to go. It's not fair that I have to miss the concert when I'm the one who wants to go the most. I don't know what my parents' problem is. Why can't they let me do anything? Why do they have to have control over everything? I don't get why they see the worst in everything. How often do people really die in terrible accidents? Not that often. Have I ever been a kid who took drugs or did really bad stuff? No! I'm always good. I get good grades. I hardly have any fun at all. Is that what they want? That I should have no fun 'til I'm, like, forty? You guys don't understand. I tried everything. I asked. I explained why this is important. I begged! I tried to make them understand. But they just don't get it! It's like—I think they were born old. They just cannot understand how going to this concert is important. They just refuse to see the possibility that I could go to something like this and not get high, maimed, or kidnapped. Why is that so hard to understand?

JEFF: I didn't want to have to tell you this, but your parents are lame. And I can say that because my parents are lame, too. The thing is that you have to control them better. Don't let them run your life! Especially when there's no harm in what you're doing, like you said. We're not doing anything bad. We're listening to music. People do that. It's been known to happen. And it's historic that parents never like what kids listen to. They think it's dangerous. Except that makes no sense, we know that.

How can music influence you, really? And do we really care *that* much about it? In a way yes, and in a way no. We like how it sounds. It doesn't run our lives. We're intelligent. We think for ourselves. If a song says, "I love donkeys" are we going to love donkeys? I don't think so. So this argument is insulting and stupid. This is why we have to take control. We see things more clearly. We're more rational. We know what we're likely to do and what we're not. It's reasonable to lie to your parents. You know you're not going to drink or get high. You know you're not going to get into a stranger's van. You're too old for that, for Pete's sake. Teddy's dad is going to drive carefully. So what could happen? Nothing. So what's the harm in lying? None.

HARRIS: He makes a good point. You know more about what you are going to do or not do. You know what you can handle. And you said yourself that you're not stupid or a kid. What's the harm in telling a little lie or two?

TEDDY: I was hoping to have a beer.

HARRIS: No one's going to sell you a beer.

JEFF: We're just going to listen to music. Big deal.

HARRIS: Don't be a loser, Liam.

LIAM: OK, OK! If we can think of a good lie, I'll tell it. I want to go to this concert.

TEDDY: I've got an idea.

JEFF: That's nice, Teddy.

TEDDY: Come on! Give me a chance.

HARRIS: No way.

TEDDY: Come on!

JEFF: OK, Teddy, shoot.

LIAM: Come on; let's be serious.

TEDDY: I am being serious! I have a good idea.

HARRIS: Please.

JEFF: Go on, go on.

TEDDY: Thanks, *Jeff*. Don't you have an older brother, Harris?

HARRIS: Yeah. So?

TEDDY: So? How old is he?

HARRIS: Nineteen.

TEDDY: So what if we said he's going with us?

(Beat.)

JEFF: That's not bad, Teddy. Not bad at all.

TEDDY: Told you. Ye of little faith . . .

LIAM: But my parents will probably say that he's even more likely to get high and take drugs.

JEFF: But if we've got Harris's brother *and* Teddy's dad—what if we said that his brother is twenty-five?

LIAM: That might work better.

HARRIS: But he's not.

JEFF: Do your parents know Harris's family?

LIAM: Not really.

TEDDY: So we're set.

LIAM: I guess so.

JEFF: Gentlemen, we are all going to the best concert of the year.

HARRIS: Excellent.

Scene 2: Forgotten

LIAM: I can't believe we were actually at the greatest concert of all time. We actually witnessed it—live!

HARRIS: I can't believe you actually managed to get here at all.

LIAM: Neither can I. I didn't think my parents would fall for that story about your twenty-five-year-old brother coming with us.

TEDDY: I knew it would work. It was my idea.

JEFF: You didn't think it would work.

TEDDY: I hoped it might.

HARRIS: That's not the same.

TEDDY: Close enough.

HARRIS: Teddy, where's your dad?

TEDDY: How am I supposed to know?

LIAM: He knows he has to pick us up, right?

TEDDY: Yeah.

JEFF: So where is he?

TEDDY: Stuck in traffic or something, I guess.

LIAM: My phone is ringing!

HARRIS: So?

LIAM: So it's my parents.

JEFF: So answer it.

LIAM: But what if they ask questions?

JEFF: So answer them. What's the big deal, Liam?

(LIAM answers his cell phone.)

LIAM: Hi? Oh. Wait a minute. He's . . . he's talking to Harris. Just a second.

(LIAM covers the phone with his hand.)

LIAM: You guys! My mom wants to speak to Harris's brother!

JEFF: Harris, pretend to be your brother.

HARRIS: How?

JEFF: Just try to sound older.

LIAM: I knew this would happen!

HARRIS: Take it easy, Liam.

(HARRIS takes the phone.)

HARRIS: *(In a deep voice.)* Hello? No problem. Don't worry about it. That's OK. I really have to . . .

(HARRIS covers the phone with his hand.)

HARRIS: His parents want my brother to stop by the house so they can thank him.

TEDDY: But . . . how are we going to do that?

HARRIS: I thought you were the mastermind, Teddy.

TEDDY: Well, sometimes I am. Can't you just say no?

HARRIS: I tried to. They won't take no for an answer.

LIAM: I am so dead. I will never see the outside of my house for the rest of my life.

JEFF: Just say you have a test to study for.

HARRIS: I'm supposed to be twenty-five though, aren't I?

LIAM: Yeah, that's what I told them.

JEFF: So say you have to go home to your kids.

HARRIS: Do I have kids?

TEDDY: My phone is ringing!

JEFF: Answer it.

(HARRIS takes his hand from the phone while TEDDY answers his cell phone.)

HARRIS: I have to go home to my kids. Thanks, though.

TEDDY: Hello? Dad?

HARRIS: Yeah. Um, two of them.

TEDDY: What?

HARRIS: They're, uh, five and seven.

TEDDY: What are we supposed to do?

HARRIS: Yeah, I did get married young.

TEDDY: We could try, but . . .

HARRIS: My wife is with them now. She's, uh, pretty. Real pretty.

TEDDY: Can't you get here? We were depending on you.

LIAM: Your dad isn't coming?

HARRIS: Sure, here he is.

TEDDY: OK. OK. Bye.

(HARRIS hands LIAM the phone.)

LIAM: Everything's great, Mom. See you soon.

(LIAM and TEDDY both hang up their phones.)

HARRIS: So what's going on, Teddy?

TEDDY: My dad's not coming.

LIAM: What?

TEDDY: His car broke down. He said we should stick together and call someone else's parents to pick us up.

LIAM: Well, we can't call my parents!

JEFF: Obviously.

HARRIS: My parents are probably asleep.

JEFF: My mom is working.

LIAM: We have to call your parents, Harris.

HARRIS: We can't.

TEDDY: Why?

HARRIS: I told them your dad was coming with us to the whole concert.

JEFF: Looks like we have to call Liam's parents.

LIAM: What? That makes no sense. No way can we call them. They'll kill me. I'm sure Harris's parents will be much more understanding.

HARRIS: Are you kidding? No way can we call my parents to pick us up. Absolutely no way. I'll never hear the end of it. I'm already the stupid kid in the family. This will be the worst thing ever. "Your brother would never do anything this stupid. Your brother's never done anything wrong in his whole entire life. Your brother was always so responsible. Your brother got excellent grades in school and never got in trouble. How come you can't be like that?" That's all I'll hear for the rest of my life. It's all I hear now! I can't even imagine how it could get worse, all the nagging, but I know somehow it will be. So I am telling you with total and absolute seriousness that there is no way on the face of the earth that I am calling my parents to pick us up.

JEFF: Deal with it, Harris.

HARRIS: I can't deal with it.

JEFF: Calm down.

HARRIS: I am calm. I'm always calm! Don't I seem calm now? Don't even answer that. I know I am! Why am I the one who has to do this? Listen to me closely. Read my lips. *I am not calling my parents to pick us up!* No! So you can just forget it. It's not going to happen.

LIAM: But my parents think your older brother is with us *right now.*

TEDDY: He has a point.

JEFF: Can't your dad still find a way here, Teddy?

TEDDY: No. His car won't start, dude.

LIAM: Could we take a taxi?

JEFF: How much money do we have?

HARRIS: It's going to be really expensive.

TEDDY: Oh my God, my wallet's gone!

LIAM: What?

TEDDY: Someone stole my wallet! It had fifty bucks

in it—all I have in the world! I cannot believe—How could this happen? I was careful!

JEFF: You brought fifty bucks with you?

TEDDY: I had fifty bucks in case I wanted to buy stuff. Like I wanted to buy a T-shirt and a beer.

JEFF: No one's going to sell you beer.

TEDDY: I know no one was going to sell me a beer, but I wanted to try! Why do you think I've been trying to grow a beard for the last month?

HARRIS: You've been trying to grow a beard?

TEDDY: OK, it wasn't working, but I was trying! And I think it's finally getting started, but not soon enough to buy a beer. But enough about the beer! My wallet with my whole life savings is missing! I need that! I was going to buy things. *(Depressed.)* I can't believe it. All gone. Everything. I just can't believe it. I was so careful. I needed that money!

JEFF: That was dumb.

TEDDY: Shut up! That really helps, Jeff! Thanks for the great insight. I just lost my wallet! It was *stolen*. So how am I the dumb one here? I'm a victim of a crime, dude!

HARRIS: That would have paid for a taxi.

TEDDY: Like I would have given you all I have in the world anyway.

HARRIS: Well, it's your fault we're in this position.

TEDDY: How is it my fault?

HARRIS: Your dad was supposed to pick us up.

TEDDY: It's my fault that my dad's car broke down? My dad is the only cool parent among us. And now you're blaming me and him for this happening? If it weren't for him, we wouldn't have gotten to the concert in the first place! That is really shabby, Harris. Not to mention that I lost my wallet! I don't care about you right now. Maybe you could help me try to find it? That might actually be helpful.

HARRIS: If you won't let us use your money to get home, why should I help you find it?

TEDDY: You really suck, Harris.

LIAM: Let's retrace your steps, Teddy.

TEDDY: I was inside, then I was here.

LIAM: But you got a drink, a Coke, right?

TEDDY: Right. I had my wallet then. And I went to the bathroom.

LIAM: Let's go look.

TEDDY: Come on, guys.

JEFF: I'm not going back in there. It's chaos.

TEDDY: We're supposed to stick together.

HARRIS: I'm staying out here with Jeff.

LIAM: Let's just go look quickly, Teddy. It won't take long.

TEDDY: We still don't know how we're going to get home.

JEFF: We'll figure it out.

HARRIS: We will?

JEFF: Sure.

LIAM: OK. We'll be back soon.

(LIAM and TEDDY exit.)

HARRIS: How are we going to get home?

JEFF: Dunno.

HARRIS: So why did you say that?

JEFF: To get them off our backs.

HARRIS: Oh. Good idea. So . . . what are we going to tell them when they get back?

JEFF: Maybe they'll find Teddy's wallet, then we'll use his money.

HARRIS: But he won't give it to us.

JEFF: Sure he will.

HARRIS: Do you really think they'll find it?

JEFF: No.

HARRIS: So we're still at square one.

JEFF: Listen, I got something from a guy here.

HARRIS: What's that?

JEFF: Weed.

HARRIS: Are you serious?

JEFF: Yeah. Want some?

HARRIS: I guess. What does it do exactly?

JEFF: Calms you down.

HARRIS: You've had it before?

JEFF: Yeah. Want some?

HARRIS: I guess.

JEFF: Come on. We just can't stand in the open like this.

(HARRIS and JEFF exit. After a second, TEDDY and LIAM reenter.)

TEDDY: I can't believe they wouldn't even let us inside to look! What am I supposed to do?

LIAM: I can't believe that guy spilled his beer on me. My parents are going to think I had one now.

TEDDY: I have to find my wallet!

LIAM: Listen, Teddy, I think your wallet's probably gone anyway. Maybe Jeff and Harris worked out a way we can get home. At this point, I just want to get home. I don't even care how.

TEDDY: Weren't we here before?

LIAM: I thought so.

TEDDY: Where are Jeff and Harris then?

LIAM: I don't know.

TEDDY: Great. What are we going to do now?

LIAM: Do you think they got a ride home without us?

TEDDY: They wouldn't do that, would they?

LIAM: Where does your mom live, Teddy?

TEDDY: Oregon.

LIAM: So I guess we can't call her for a ride.

TEDDY: It would take her a really, really, really long time to get here.

LIAM: I guess . . . I guess we have no choice. We have to call my parents.

TEDDY: There must be another way.

LIAM: What? I wish there were.

TEDDY: What are you going to tell them?

LIAM: Maybe I can sort of tell them the truth. I could say that Harris's older brother took Harris and Jeff home, and we were supposed to go home with your father instead, but then your father's car broke down.

TEDDY: That's good.

LIAM: It's worth a try.

(JEFF and HARRIS enter.)

HARRIS: Where's the wallet?

TEDDY: Where have you been?

LIAM: We thought you went home.

JEFF: No.

TEDDY: You smell.

(HARRIS and JEFF laugh.)

LIAM: Now what are we going to do? I'm coated in beer, and they're high.

TEDDY: Let's face it. We're doomed.

TALK BACK!

1. If you were in Liam's situation in Scene 1, what would you do?

2. What would be important enough to you so you'd lie or do whatever you needed to do to get what you want?

3. What's the worst thing that could happen to the guys at the end of the play?

4. Do you think the concert was worth the consequences? Why or why not?

5. Are you influenced a lot by peer pressure? Why or why not?

6. Among your friends, are you a person who goes with the flow or makes the rules?

7. What would be the best way for the boys to solve their dilemma at the end of Scene 2?

PUZZLE

1F, 4M

WHO

FEMALES   MALES
  Elizabeth   B
                               M
                               R
                               V

WHERE A white room.

WHEN The near future.

Be very clear in both scenes about where your character is in terms of belief/rebellion. Decide as a group what characteristics the brainwashed characters exhibit. Do they walk or talk differently? Elizabeth needs to appear completely kind and trustworthy.

It's great when you have no limits on sets, props, and costumes, but many theaters don't have enough money. Write a play where all you can have onstage is a table and two chairs. One character has to wear jeans and a T-shirt. Another character has to wear a suit. Your only props are a pen, a feather, a sneaker, and a plastic bag.

Scene 1: Place

ELIZABETH: How are you this morning?

M: Fine.

ELIZABETH: Good. It's a beautiful day.

M: Is it? How do you know?

ELIZABETH: I just know. You need to trust me.

M: I do. I just still don't understand how you decide what's beautiful and what's not. Especially when you can't see it.

ELIZABETH: Keep trying. One day you'll understand.

M: I try every day, and it doesn't get any easier. Yesterday you said it would be a beautiful day, but I had to go see the doctors.

ELIZABETH: Was it really so bad?

M: I don't know. I never know. They don't talk to me. But I always feel like it's bad.

ELIZABETH: Why?

M: Because they don't talk to me. But they talk to each other in serious voices. It makes me nervous.

ELIZABETH: You mustn't be nervous. They're only trying to help you.

M: But what do I need help with? I feel fine.

ELIZABETH: The doctors know best. It's better not to ask questions.

M: Why?

ELIZABETH: Like I said, you need to learn to trust.

M: But why? What if I don't want to trust?

ELIZABETH: Maybe you should see the doctors again. You seem very agitated today.

M: No! I'm fine. I'm fine. I won't ask more questions.

ELIZABETH: We all want what's best for you. You know that, don't you?

M: I guess so.

ELIZABETH: Do you think I would put you through anything unnecessary? Do you think I want to see you harmed?

M: No.

ELIZABETH: Of course not. I want only the best for you. The doctors are the same.

M: It doesn't seem like it sometimes, that's all.

ELIZABETH: Then you must trust me.

M: What do they tell you? About me, I mean.

ELIZABETH: They tell me you are doing well most of the

time. Sometimes you just get too anxious. You get rebellious. You talk back. You know this.

M: I do. But . . .

ELIZABETH: See? You mustn't do that.

M: Why can't I disagree? Why can't I want to know? If someone would just answer that maybe I wouldn't—

ELIZABETH: Trust. You must learn to trust.

M: Why, Elizabeth? I just want to know the answer to this one question.

ELIZABETH: It's the one answer you'll never get, I'm afraid. Now it's puzzle time. The others will be coming soon.

(There is a knock at the door.)

ELIZABETH: Just on time! Come in!

H: We're here, Elizabeth.

ELIZABETH: Get your puzzles and sit down.

(H, M, B, and R get workbooks.)

ELIZABETH: When you're ready, you may begin. I'll be outside.

(ELIZABETH exits. H, M, B, and R settle down to work on the workbooks. After a beat, R throws his workbook across the room.)

B: They're going to come in now.

R: I hate puzzle time.

B: They're going to come in now. Pick it up!

R: No.

H: Just pretend.

R: I don't want to.

M: Do you think there's a reason we have to do them?

B: You're not supposed to ask questions.

H: I think there is a reason.

M: What is it?

R: There's no reason. We're being tortured.

H: There has to be a reason.

M: What could it be?

H: I don't know.

B: Be quiet! I don't want to hear this.

R: He's been like this ever since the last time he went to the doctors. What did they do to you?

B: No questions!

R: You used to ask questions.

B: No questions.

H: Do you—draw what they did to you.

(B starts to draw.)

R: I remember something.

M: What?

R: I remember the sun.

H: It doesn't exist.

M: I remember that the day means something, but I don't know what. I can't understand how Elizabeth can know it's a beautiful day.

R: Because of the sun.

H: You just found that in a book.

R: A book they didn't want me to find.

M: How did you find it?

R: My nurse left it in her bag.

H: How come they didn't come in?

(R, H, and M freeze, looking out at the audience and listening.)

M: I don't hear anything.

H: Maybe they're not watching.

R: They're always watching.

H: We should pretend to work.

R: What are we doing this for?

B: No questions!

H: Are you done? I mean, show me your picture.

(B shows H what he drew.)

H: The usual. Doctors talking.

M: That's it?

B: NO QUESTIONS!

R: They brainwashed him. He'll be like this for a while. Put your heads down for a minute. Act like you're working on a puzzle.

(B, M, and H look down at their workbooks. R picks up his workbook and takes up the same attitude.)

R: I'm remembering things. The sun. Colors like blue. I know I'm not supposed to be here. None of us are. In this book I read, they go to the beach. I think I know what this is. I think I remember the taste of it. Salt. In the air and in the water and on the food. I was there. I know it. And I'm not supposed to be here. I think I belong somewhere else. Also . . . also in this book, people ask questions.

B: No questions.

R: They ask questions all the time. They wonder about things out loud, and people answer them. They just answer them. They don't tell them that they need to trust or they need to get older or they need to do something else first. They just tell them. Or they try to.

H: But that's a book. It's imaginary.

R: What if the book isn't fake? What if that book is what's real? What if we're trapped in a false world here?

(B opens his mouth to speak.)

R: Do your puzzles! Don't speak!

(B returns to his puzzles.)

R: Don't you have little moments where you feel like there's more out there? That there are things you almost . . . that there's just more trying to come to the surface? I feel like I'm hitting my head against the wall all the time. Like there's something in there I need to recall. Something important. I think I'm getting close.

M: Elizabeth tells me that people are unkind when you ask questions. That it's better to trust. There are things I don't want to know. Trusting is better; it makes you happier. But I don't see why. Every answer leads to a new question. I . . . I just don't see why questions are so bad. Or answers. Or knowing! How can it be so bad to know? So I get worried. I get anxious. Then I have to go to the doctor because I get anxious. And I get even more anxious when I have to go to the doctors and they whisper about me and I can't hear them. I want to know. I wouldn't be anxious if I knew. What are they saying? Why am I here? Why are we doing all this? What's going on? If they would just tell me, I'd be happier, I think. I just don't like not knowing. I don't like it. I want to know. And if Elizabeth cares for me like she says she does, if she's watching out for my welfare, why won't she tell me anything? I think something bad is going on.

R: I heard the doctors say something. I heard—

H: Quiet! Someone's coming!

(R, M, and H stare out ahead of them, listening.)

B: I'm done!

(Beat. ELIZABETH enters, as cheerful as before.)

ELIZABETH: *(To B.)* You're going to take a nap! *(To R.)* You're coming with me.

R: I don't want to come with you.

ELIZABETH: Everything's going to be all right.

R: No, it's not!

ELIZABETH: You're worrying the others. Everything is going to be fine. I promise. Now come with me.

R: No!

(ELIZABETH whispers to B. B stands beside R.)

ELIZABETH: Come with me.

R: No!

> *(R begins to walk away, but B holds his arm as ELIZABETH quickly pokes his arm with some sort of device. R falls to the floor almost immediately.)*

ELIZABETH: *(To M, H, and B.)* See? Everything's going to be fine.

Scene 2: Time

ELIZABETH: Puzzle time!

H: Here we are, Elizabeth.

ELIZABETH: Good. Sit down and get started.

>   *(H, B, M, and R get out their workbooks. R and B work furiously.)*

M: *(To R.)* What happened to you yesterday when they took you away?

>   *(R seems not to hear M.)*

B: No questions.

M: What do you remember?

>   *(R still does not respond to M.)*

M: Can you hear me?

B: No questions!

M: Can you say something else for once?

>   *(B stands up and walks over to M.)*

B: No questions.

M: *(Standing.)* Or what?

B: No questions.

(M pushes B.)

M: Or what? I'll end up like you?

B: No questions!

H: Stop it! That's exactly what's going to happen and you know it! Calm down—quick! They're going to come in here.

(M calms down and sits. B sits as well.)

M: What are they doing to us? What did they do to him? *(Indicates R.)* He was fine yesterday.

H: He remembered something. And he heard something he wasn't supposed to.

M: How come you stay so normal?

H: I've been here a long time. I know how it works.

M: How long?

H: I don't know. How could I? They decide what we do and when we do it. They decide if it's light or dark. I think they keep us confused on purpose. I think they change things all the time to keep us off balance. I think some days are a few hours long, and other days are very, very long.

M: Why would they do that?

H: I don't know exactly. I think they're testing us somehow.

M: Why?

H: You do ask a lot of questions.

M: Why not?

H: Because it gets you turned into those guys. *(Indicates B and R.)*

M: Why do we need to do puzzles all the time?

H: Can you keep calm?

M: Yes.

H: Can you keep quiet?

M: Yes. You know something, don't you?

H: Can you keep what I'm going to say between us?

M: Yes—what is it?

H: This is just a theory.

M: Whatever!

H: OK. **I think that we're being experimented on.**

M: That's what I was thinking!

H: **Shhh! But there's more.**

M: What more?

H: I also think that maybe we're also doing their calculations.

M: Calculations?

H: Well, I don't know exactly what their experiments are—maybe they're to do with intelligence or sense deprivation or behavior or brainwashing—but I think that maybe we're figuring out for them what they need to do next. That these "puzzles" are either chemical calculations or they're a test to see how we're affected by their experiments. Or both!

M: You're kidding.

H: Why would I kid about that?

M: Good question. I don't know.

H: I wouldn't. I think they try to make this seem like fun and games, these puzzles they give us, but somehow they relate back to the experiments the doctors are doing.

M: Then I'm not going to do them anymore!

H: No! Then they'll know that we're onto them.

M: But we can't let them do this to us!

H: Shhh! I know! So I've been thinking about what to do. I think one of us should purposely mess up our calculations. But the other one can't. That person needs to be a witness. If we seem dumber is that better or worse? Will we get left alone? Treated better or worse?

M: It's a good idea.

H: You see why just one of us needs to do it.

M: In case you get made into one of them. *(Indicates B and R.)*

H: Right. **So which one of us should it be?**

(ELIZABETH enters.)

ELIZABETH: Is everybody OK in here?

H: Yes, Elizabeth.

ELIZABETH: Because I heard a commotion in here.

H: Everything's OK.

M: It was an accident.

B: He asked a question.

M: It was an accident. Sorry.

ELIZABETH: What did I tell you about asking questions?

B: No questions!

ELIZABETH: I was asking him.

B: *(To ELIZABETH.)* No asking questions!

ELIZABETH: Oh, I see. It's OK for me to ask him this one little question.

B: Oh.

ELIZABETH: Well? What did I tell you?

M: You told me not to ask questions.

ELIZABETH: What should you do instead?

M: Trust you. And I do.

ELIZABETH: Good. Because you should. You can always trust me. I only want what's best for you.

M: OK.

ELIZABETH: OK then. Since we're all getting along, let's get back to our puzzles. And no talking.

(ELIZABETH exits.)

M: You're so polite to her.

H: Have to be.

M: Why?

H: She's not as nice as she seems.

M: Sure she is.

H: She's on their side.

M: Are you sure?

H: Shhh. I'm totally sure. So, do you agree with me? About doing the work wrong today?

M: OK. It makes sense.

H: Which one of us should it be?

M: You!

H: Why me?

M: I don't want to be an idiot.

H: Neither do I!

M: It was your idea.

H: Exactly. I think I know a little bit better how to work this system. Elizabeth doesn't suspect me. I've been here longer. She trusts me. Or, should I say, she trusts that I trust her. You're one step away from being dragged off to see the doctors again anyway, and you know what that means.

M: I am not going to get taken to the doctors like these guys.

H: You got into a fight with Brainwashed Boy just a few minutes ago!

M: That was all him.

H: They won't see it like that.

(Beat while M thinks.)

M: I don't want to. But . . . OK. I'll do it.

H: Things might get even better. They might see you as less of a threat.

M: Just in case I get turned into—in case I come back without a memory—can I tell you some things?

H: Sure.

M: Will you try to remind me of them later? I don't really want to forget.

H: OK.

M: I want to remember . . . that I ask a lot of questions. That I'm curious. That I don't like to do what I'm told. I want to remember that I don't like broccoli. I write with my right hand. I don't floss. I pretend I do, but I don't. When I'm being silly, I flare my nostrils. In my head, I call Elizabeth MaryAnn. I heard that name once and that's what she looks like her name should be to me. And I call myself Mike. I know us boys are not supposed to use names, but I do. I name everyone.

H: What's my name?

M: You're Dennis.

H: Dennis?

M: Don't you like it?

H: I guess it's OK.

M: You look like a Dennis to me.

H: OK. Are you sure about this?

M: No. I don't want to do this. But I do want to know. So I'll do it anyway. Oh, one last thing. Will you remind me that I did this? I want to think that maybe even in a small way I was a little bit brave.

H: You are. I'll make sure you know it. If I can.

M: OK, then. Thanks.

H: Thank you for . . . you know.

M: Here we go . . .

(M and H go back to filling in their workbooks.)

TALK BACK!

1. What do you think is the objective of the doctors in this play?

2. How do the doctors try to control the behavior of the boys?

3. Would you trust Elizabeth? Why do you think Elizabeth works for the doctors?

4. What do you think happens to the boys when they get sent to the doctors?

5. Would you do what M does at the end of the play? Do you think he's brave or stupid?

6. Bad people think what they're doing is right and good. Do you think this is true or false?

THE INITIATION

6F, 5M

WHO
    FEMALES   MALES
      Arielle   Drake
      Danielle   Erol
      Janelle   Hadrian
      Laurie   Isaak
      Noelle   Steve
      Rochelle

WHERE A school hallway.

WHEN Present day.

🎭 The Elles: Do an activity together without Laurie. Don't tell her anything about what you did. Discuss afterward how this activity made you feel. See if you can incorporate your discoveries into your characters.

✍ Turn this play on its head. What if, say, the nerds, the class clowns, the unathletic kids, or the heavy metal fans ruled the school? How would they decide who gets into their group? What might their initiation be like?

Scene 1: The Elles

ARIELLE: Your hair is all wrong.

LAURIE: How should it be?

NOELLE: Just different.

ROCHELLE: Not how it is.

LAURIE: Tell me how it should be, and I'll get it done how you want.

JANELLE: It just needs to be completely different.

DANIELLE: Up-to-date. Like, modern.

LAURIE: OK. I'll get my hair cut this weekend.

ARIELLE: Oh! That reminds me. This weekend the guys are coming to my house.

NOELLE: Oh my God!

ROCHELLE: Which guys?

ARIELLE: The usual suspects: Hadrian, Isaak, Erol, Steve, Drake.

JANELLE: Can I just say now, Drake is mine?

DANIELLE: I like Drake, too.

JANELLE: You can have Isaak.

NOELLE: Isaak is mine.

LAURIE: Which one do I get? Hadrian?

NOELLE: Oh my God!

ROCHELLE: What do you mean?

LAURIE: I mean, which guy do I get? I don't want to pick one that one of you already has dibs on.

ARIELLE: You don't get one.

LAURIE: Why not?

DANIELLE: You haven't done the initiation.

JANELLE: Plus, we didn't invite you.

LAURIE: Oh. I thought . . . What's the initiation?

NOELLE: We all went through it.

ROCHELLE: It's exactly what we said. It's an initiation.

ARIELLE: Into the group.

DANIELLE: We've never had a member that wasn't an Elle, though.

LAURIE: What does that mean?

JANELLE: Janelle, Danielle, Arielle—we're all Elles.

ROCHELLE: We even call ourselves that. The Elles.

LAURIE: So does that mean I can't be a member?

ARIELLE: Well . . . we could make an exception. Except . . .

LAURIE: What?

ARIELLE: I just think the initiation should be a little harder, that's all.

LAURIE: That's fine with me!

NOELLE: You wouldn't mind?

DANIELLE: You'd have to do everything we say . . .

ROCHELLE: And if you don't . . .

ARIELLE: You're out.

LAURIE: Just tell me what to do. Please?

ARIELLE: Should we, girls?

JANELLE: I say no.

LAURIE: Please? I'll do whatever you want.

NOELLE: I say let her try.

ROCHELLE: I agree with Noelle.

DANIELLE: I agree with Rochelle.

ARIELLE: And I *(Pausing for suspense.)* . . . agree, too. Janelle?

JANELLE: I guess. If she's willing to do whatever . . .

LAURIE: I am! I swear!

JANELLE: Well then . . .

ARIELLE: We're agreed. You're going to go through the initiation. You're very lucky. We've turned down a bunch of girls. Nancy Turner? Reagan Simone? Lia Masterson? We turned down all of them. They just didn't have it. We're looking for something more than just the ordinary girl. Just anyone won't do. You need to be well dressed, pretty, not stupid, not geeky, and willing to break the rules. We don't like to follow other people's rules. Of course, it can't be anarchy. We have rules of our own. Like always have lip gloss and a short skirt in your bag. Like always help a sister with a test or homework. That's a good example. Teachers and parents say, "Don't cheat." Well, let's face it. We do. But we see it as helping. As a sign of sisterhood. Which is better: Helping someone or letting them fail? Definitely helping them, right? So that's how we operate. We stick together. So we all succeed in the end. If that means breaking the rules, so what? Is this something you're up for?

LAURIE: Definitely! I just know we'll be friends.

JANELLE: Just remember that you promised to do whatever we want.

LAURIE: Like what would that be, anyway?

ARIELLE: You'll see . . .

LAURIE: Can you give me a hint?

DANIELLE: The guys are coming over here!

(HADRIAN, ISAAK, EROL, STEVE, and DRAKE enter.)

HADRIAN: Hey.

ARIELLE: Hey. So, you're coming to my house on Saturday night.

HADRIAN: I guess.

ARIELLE: You said you would.

HADRIAN: I'll be there.

JANELLE: And the rest of you guys?

STEVE: I guess.

DANIELLE: Drake?

JANELLE: Drake, I was hoping you'd be there.

(DANIELLE shoots JANELLE the evil eye.)

DRAKE: Whatever.

EROL: I thought we were hanging at Steve's.

STEVE: Whatever.

ISAAK: We could stop by.

NOELLE: You should. It'll be fun.

ISAAK: Promise?

ARIELLE: Definitely.

HADRIAN: OK, well. Bye.

ARIELLE: Later.

(HADRIAN, ISAAK, STEVE, EROL, and DRAKE exit.)

ARIELLE: I just got an idea.

DANIELLE: What?

ARIELLE: Laurie's first task in the initiation.

LAURIE: What?

ARIELLE: Two words: Kiss Erol.

LAURIE: What?

NOELLE: You heard her.

JANELLE: You said you'd do anything.

LAURIE: Well . . . which one is Erol?

ARIELLE: The one walking back this way.

LAURIE: Now?

ROCHELLE: Next week. No, of course now!

LAURIE: Well, what should I . . .

ARIELLE: Just do it, or you can forget about coming Saturday.

LAURIE: If I do this, I can come Saturday?

ARIELLE: Maybe.

(EROL enters.)

LAURIE: OK.

ARIELLE: Oh, one more thing.

LAURIE: What?

ARIELLE: On the lips.

LAURIE: Are you serious?

ARIELLE: For ten seconds.

LAURIE: Are you serious?

JANELLE: Those are the rules.

LAURIE: Well . . .

DANIELLE: If you can't handle it . . .

NOELLE: The rest of us went through the initiation . . .

LAURIE: OK, OK! I'll do it.

(LAURIE walks over to EROL as the ELLES watch.)

LAURIE: Hi.

EROL: Uh, hi.

LAURIE: I was with those girls? The Elles? Just a minute ago? Anyhow, I'm sort of going to be one of them, part of the group, which is very exciting. Except, see, I have to do some things first. So I can join. It's like an initiation. I need to prove myself. And I kind of need your help with something. It'll only take a second. Oh, I know you don't know me, so, hi! I'm Laurie.

EROL: Yeah, hi.

(EROL starts to walk away.)

LAURIE: So I was thinking! About you and me!

EROL: You and me?

LAURIE: I was thinking . . . maybe we could . . .

EROL: I gotta go.

LAURIE: Kiss! Maybe we should kiss.

EROL: What?

LAURIE: There's this initiation and I'm supposed to kiss you. On the lips. It's kind of a dare. I have to just do it. It's nothing personal. I'm not trying to . . . you know. I just need to do this. For ten seconds.

EROL: I don't think so.

LAURIE: Why not?

EROL: I don't know you.

LAURIE: I'm Laurie, remember? Listen, please, I know this is weird, but it's for the initiation, and it's really important to me. And they're looking right now. This is only the first task, and I have to get this right. Please!

EROL: It's not important to me.

LAURIE: Look, I've got an idea. I need to look like I've kissed you on the lips for ten seconds. So I could put my hand over your mouth when I do it, right? Then it won't be like a kiss at all. But no one will know except us.

EROL: But I don't know you.

LAURIE: Please.

EROL: Maybe I don't want to kiss you.

LAURIE: Why? It wouldn't be real.

EROL: But people might think it was.

LAURIE: But—they would think *I* kissed *you*. Please?

(Beat.)

EROL: I guess.

LAURIE: You will? Really? That's . . . great. So I guess . . . We should just do it, right? OK. Um, it has to look real to them. Let me put my back to them so they don't see.

EROL: Whatever.

LAURIE: OK. I guess I'm going to kiss you now—I mean, not really kiss you, but you know . . .

EROL: I don't have all day.

LAURIE: OK. Here we go.

Scene 2: First Dare

(As the ELLES watch, LAURIE appears to be kissing EROL, with her back to the audience and the girls. She holds this position for ten seconds.)

DANIELLE: I can't believe she actually did it.

(HADRIAN enters.)

JANELLE: What a sucker.

HADRIAN: What a slut!

ROCHELLE: She really *will* do anything we dare her to do.

ARIELLE: I knew this would be fun.

(LAURIE walks over to the ELLES.)

LAURIE: So? How did I do?

DANIELLE: That was pretty good.

JANELLE: That's only the first dare, remember?

ARIELLE: There are lots more to come.

LAURIE: How many more?

ARIELLE: Lots. You'll see. Saturday is going to be so fun.

NOELLE: I can't wait.

DANIELLE: It's going to be awesome.

ARIELLE: Come on, girls.

(The ELLES exit with LAURIE following.)

JANELLE: What are you doing?

LAURIE: Coming with you.

ROCHELLE: You need to walk behind us.

JANELLE: You're not one of us yet.

LAURIE: OK.

ARIELLE: Bye, Hadrian.

(The ELLES exit with LAURIE following a few paces behind. HADRIAN walks over to EROL.)

HADRIAN: Man, that girl was all over you! What was up with that?

EROL: Dunno.

HADRIAN: What a slut! They said she's going to be at the party on Saturday. That will be good. So are you going to go after her?

EROL: I dunno.

HADRIAN: Well, if you don't, I will.

(STEVE, ISAAK, and DRAKE enter.)

ISAAK: What are you standing around for? We have practice.

HADRIAN: You guys, this girl just grabbed Erol in the hallway and practically sucked his face off.

STEVE: Are you serious? That never happens to me.

ISAAK: What did she do it for?

HADRIAN: She was totally hot for him.

DRAKE: Who was it?

EROL: I don't know. I think she said her name was Laurie.

ISAAK: You don't even know her?

EROL: No.

STEVE: Was she ugly?

EROL: No.

HADRIAN: You should have seen them going at it. Man, what a slut!

DRAKE: So, what do you think of her?

EROL: I dunno. I don't think anything.

HADRIAN: What's wrong with you? I told him that if he didn't want her, I'm going after her.

DRAKE: Hey, if she's that into you, Erol, it would be a crime to let that get by you.

STEVE: It's a chance of a lifetime.

ISAAK: Maybe he's not into her.

HADRIAN: Are you into her?

EROL: I dunno. I hadn't thought about it.

STEVE: So think about it now! Are you gonna do her?

EROL: I don't even know her.

HADRIAN: That's it. You had your chance. She's mine now.

ISAAK: I thought you were into Arielle.

HADRIAN: She's into me. I can take her or leave her.

DRAKE: But she's popular. We don't know who this Laurie is.

HADRIAN: But we know what she does.

EROL: It wasn't really anything.

STEVE: Don't be modest, Erol.

ISAAK: We should find out more about her.

HADRIAN: What more do we need to know? Let's look at the facts. This Laurie girl walked up to our friend Erol and just kissed him. Stuck her tongue down his throat. Was totally all over him. Out of nowhere! So what can we conclude about that? This Laurie girl is easy. So, OK, let's say she's really into Erol, and that's why she did it. Does that mean that she wouldn't do the same thing with another guy?

Like if we told her Erol isn't into her? No. She'd do it. She's a bad girl. And girls like that are always popular in their own way. OK, so maybe you don't want to be seen with them all the time, but a little bit of contact with a girl like that can never be bad. Even if she's not the best-looking or most popular person, she definitely has a purpose, know what I mean? So I think we focus on what's important about her. She's ready, willing, and able. And if Erol's not going to take advantage of that, I will.

STEVE: Why you? Why not me?

HADRIAN: Because I said it first. I have dibs. Let's get to practice.

(HADRIAN, STEVE, and ISAAK exit.)

DRAKE: Was she really all over you?

EROL: Not really.

DRAKE: Do you know her?

EROL: Not until today.

DRAKE: Does she like you, do you think?

EROL: I don't know. I don't think so.

DRAKE: Why would she do that? No offense. It's just strange for a girl to do that.

EROL: I don't know. I think . . . It could have been a dare or something.

DRAKE: That would make sense. Do you think it was?

EROL: I dunno.

DRAKE: So I guess you're not into her.

EROL: I don't know her. I don't know why everyone is making such a big deal out of this. I don't know this girl. So it's all a little weird. I mean, I don't see why . . . I'm just not . . . Sometimes I don't get Hadrian and Steve.

DRAKE: They're sex obsessed or something. Yeah, I mean, I like girls and all, but I'm not *totally* obsessed or anything. I like to play it a little cool. I choose, like, a girl I like and not just any female who breathes. I mean, can you imagine making out with Martha Jeffries? She doesn't even bathe. But I bet Drake wouldn't care. He doesn't have any standards at all. I'm a teenage guy and I think guy things, you know, but I'm not an idiot. People like Hadrian make those things seem like the same thing: "I am a teenage guy, therefore, I am a total idiot." Not that I don't like girls or anything. Because I do. I sort of think this girl in my math class is cute. I mean, you stare at someone's hair long enough, and you start to wonder more about the front of them. So I talked to her the other day, and she seems nice. But that's just it. I don't think I'd like a girl who came on to me really strong. I think it would freak me out. Girls aren't supposed to act like that. They're supposed to be . . . well, we're supposed to do that, right?

EROL: Well, I guess you don't have to worry about being rejected.

DRAKE: That's true. I don't know . . .

(LAURIE enters.)

EROL: Oh no. It's that girl again.

DRAKE: Man, she really can't get enough of you. She doesn't look the way I expected her to.

(LAURIE walks up to EROL.)

LAURIE: Hi.

EROL: Hi.

LAURIE: Listen, about before I just wanted to say—

EROL: I'm not that into you.

LAURIE: What?

DRAKE: He's not that into you.

LAURIE: I don't understand.

EROL: I'm not that into you.

LAURIE: But I don't get it. I told you—

DRAKE: Sorry, but sometimes you have to take no for an answer.

(HADRIAN enters and walks up to the group.)

LAURIE: This doesn't make any sense. I never . . . What do you think . . . I told you—

HADRIAN: Hey, listen, Erol's not into you. So how about we go somewhere?

LAURIE: Like where?

HADRIAN: I don't know. We could find a place.

LAURIE: Why?

HADRIAN: You know why.

LAURIE: I do?

HADRIAN: Sure you do.

LAURIE: Look, I just wanted to say I was sorry. I know that was weird.

EROL: Whatever. No big deal.

HADRIAN: Come on. I'm going to make you the most popular girl in school.

LAURIE: How?

HADRIAN: You'll see.

TALK BACK!

1. What do you think of the Elles and the sisterhood?

2. Would you go through an initiation? Why or why not?

3. Do you like being part of a group or do you prefer being an individual? Why?

4. How and why do rumors start?

5. Who's more like the guys you know: Hadrian or Drake?

6. Would you want to go to Arielle's party? Why or why not?

7. Should Laurie leave with Hadrian at the end of Scene 2 or not? Why?

8. What do you think of girls asking guys out?

9. Could a girl get a reputation at your school for doing what Laurie did?

LOSING MY MIND

5F, 3M

WHO

FEMALES
Dakota
Fleur
Vivian
Finola
Leigh

MALES
Barry
Clark
Lucky

WHERE Scene 1: The school gym; Scene 2: Lucky's room.

WHEN Present day.

🎭 Try a "speed through" during rehearsal: say and do everything you need to do in the play, only much, much quicker. When you go back to doing the play normally, see if you can still keep the feeling of being rushed, especially in Scene 1.

✍ Imagine you've got amnesia. Everything you know about yourself—your likes and dislikes—are forgotten. You get to remake yourself. You see your family and friends with fresh eyes. How would you change your life? Write about it!

Scene 1: Slip

BARRY: What happened?

FLEUR: He slipped.

FINOLA: He was trying to show off, as usual.

LEIGH: Is he OK?

CLARK: Should I get the nurse?

BARRY: I think—He's OK. He's breathing anyway.

CLARK: I'll get the nurse.

BARRY: What was he thinking?

LEIGH: You know Lucky. Always doing something crazy.

FINOLA: He was trying to impress Leigh.

FLEUR: He likes her.

LEIGH: No, he doesn't!

FLEUR: He definitely does. He just jumped off the top of the bleachers for you.

LEIGH: I didn't ask him to. In fact, I think it's stupid.

FINOLA: He just wanted to get your attention.

LEIGH: How do you know he wasn't trying to get your attention?

FLEUR: Well, I think when he said, "Hey, Leigh, look!" that was a hint.

LEIGH: Shut up.

FLEUR: Make me.

LEIGH: It still doesn't make sense. How could anyone be impressed by someone jumping off of the bleachers?

BARRY: You weren't impressed? He jumped from pretty high up.

FINOLA: You're sure he's not dead.

BARRY: Definitely not dead. We just shouldn't move him.

FINOLA: OK.

LEIGH: Why would someone doing something stupid impress me?

BARRY: Do you all feel this way?

FLEUR: Well, it's high, but it's also very dumb.

FINOLA: I thought he was going to break his legs. I didn't want to see that happen.

BARRY: But doesn't seeing a guy do something dangerous—isn't that exciting? Especially if he's doing it for you?

LEIGH: Not so much.

BARRY: You're kidding! This changes everything. I

thought—all guys think that girls like to see guys do dangerous things. Then you're like a bad, dangerous guy. I thought girls liked that. I really did. You know, stuntmen and all that? Let me just get this straight. Girls really don't like guys doing dangerous things? It's not sexy?

FINOLA: I guess it only works if you're famous or something. I don't know.

BARRY: Ah-ha! So it is sexy when some people do dangerously stupid things but not others. What's the difference?

FLEUR: Dunno.

BARRY: You're not being very helpful. Here's another thing. OK. So here's Lucky. Unconscious. Having jumped off of the top of the bleachers to impress you. He's hurt. He's injured! We don't know what's wrong with him or if he'll live or die!

FINOLA: You said he was going to live!

BARRY: OK, I was being dramatic. He's going to live. He's not even bleeding. But let me get back to what I was saying. Now he's hurt. Don't you want to hold him close to you and cry and, like, devote your life to him getting better? Because that's what you see on TV all the time. We're meant to think that this is how women are. That all you have to do is hurt yourself in some way other than, like, getting a paper cut, and some girl will be devoted to you for life.

FLEUR: False.

LEIGH: Totally false!

FINOLA: Completely false. There would need to be some major damage, and I'd have to like the guy to begin with.

BARRY: Huh. Very interesting. This is so educational!

FLEUR: So, in other words, Finola would be devoted to *you* if *you* jumped off the bleachers.

FINOLA: Fleur! That is not true, Barry. She's on drugs. It's sad.

LEIGH: Oh sure. You don't like being made fun of, but you don't mind doing it to me.

FINOLA: I didn't do anything to you.

FLEUR: Everyone knows Lucky likes Leigh, don't they, Barry?

BARRY: Well, I don't know . . .

FLEUR: He knows. He's just not saying. It's a guy thing.

LEIGH: But why would Lucky like me? I'm always mad at him. He's always doing stupid stuff. He's been annoying me since birth, practically, pulling my pigtails and sticking straws up his nose. Remember that time he put a quarter in his nose and the nurse had to pull it out with tweezers? That was gross. Or the time he turned his eyelids inside out and couldn't get them to go back? Lucky is so gross. I'm sorry. I'm sorry if you can hear me, Lucky, but you're always doing gross things! I don't mean to be cruel, but you guys know what I mean.

FINOLA: But, come on, Leigh. Deep down you know he likes you. Pulling your pigtails? That's a classic sign that a five-year-old wants to marry you.

LEIGH: But why can't he just do normal things? Like he could carry my books or walk me home or buy me a soda at lunchtime or something. That would be normal. That would be nice. Why do guys think that irritating a person is going to get them to like you? Irritating a person is just plain irritating!

FLEUR: Yeah, Barry, how come?

BARRY: I don't know. I try not to be irritating.

FINOLA: I know.

FLEUR: See?

FINOLA: I was just . . . acknowledging him!

FLEUR: Yeah, whatever. You like him.

FINOLA: I swear, I don't, Barry. She's so drugged.

FLEUR: You wish.

LEIGH: Look! He's moving!

FINOLA: Thank God he's alive!

BARRY: I told you he was alive.

FLEUR: Do you think he'll be able to walk?

LEIGH: He's moving his legs.

(LUCKY opens his eyes and groans.)

LUCKY: Oh man, my head hurts!

LEIGH: Are you OK?

FINOLA: We were worried about you.

BARRY: This is what I was talking about!

FLEUR: Be quiet, Barry, we're talking to Lucky!

FINOLA: Can you speak, Lucky?

BARRY: He *is* speaking.

FLEUR: He's getting jealous, Finola.

FINOLA: Well, he'll have to wait. We're dealing with poor Lucky now.

LEIGH: Speak to us, Lucky. Are you in pain?

LUCKY: My head hurts.

FLEUR: Poor thing!

LEIGH: Does anything else hurt, Lucky?

BARRY: And don't say your pants.

LUCKY: My head is killing me!

FINOLA: We know.

LEIGH: I guess he's otherwise OK.

LUCKY: Where am I?

FLEUR: At school.

LUCKY: School?

LEIGH: Surely you remember school.

BARRY: I wish I could forget school.

FINOLA: Barry, do you mind? Hold the sarcasm for the moment.

BARRY: Excuse me!

(CLARK runs in.)

CLARK: The nurse is coming. She wants to know if anything's broken or if he's bleeding.

FLEUR: No.

CLARK: Can he breathe and speak?

FLEUR: Yes.

CLARK: OK!

(CLARK runs out again.)

LUCKY: Who are you people? Where am I?

Scene 2: Slide

DAKOTA: We were so worried about you!

VIVIAN: We just heard about it but we were away at Model UN so we couldn't come home until now to see you!

DAKOTA: Are you OK?

LUCKY: I don't know who anybody is. Who are you?

VIVIAN: Lucky, it's us!

CLARK: He doesn't remember anything. Lucky, these are your sisters, Vivian and Dakota. Your mom showed you pictures of them earlier.

DAKOTA: We're the twins! You have to remember us! We've known you our whole lives!

LUCKY: Right. Sure.

VIVIAN: You're lying.

LUCKY: Right. Sure.

DAKOTA: Poor brother! We'll help you remember, won't we, Vivian!

VIVIAN: We might leave out a few little bits where we don't come out so well, but the rest . . .

DAKOTA: You really don't remember anything?

LUCKY: You're giving me a headache.

VIVIAN: Well, that sounds like him at least.

DAKOTA: I'm so glad nothing's broken and he's OK.

VIVIAN: I know we've fought in the past, Lucky, but we still love you most of the time. Even though you're our annoying brother.

LUCKY: Why does everyone keep calling me Lucky?

CLARK: Well, you don't seem too lucky at the moment, do you? Ha!

DAKOTA: I'm sorry, but that wasn't funny, Clark.

CLARK: Just trying to lighten the mood.

VIVIAN: Don't.

DAKOTA: So tell us everything, Clark! And tell Lucky, too, so at least he'll remember that part of his life.

CLARK: Well, I didn't actually see it. One minute he was standing with me, next minute he's on the floor and some girls are screaming.

VIVIAN: Lucky, just so you know, you're always doing stupid things.

DAKOTA: Constantly. So, you don't know anything else?

CLARK: The girls said he jumped off the bleachers to show off.

VIVIAN: See? You're a show-off. You jumped off the bleachers at school.

LUCKY: What are bleachers?

DAKOTA: They're like steps.

LUCKY: Why would I do that?

VIVIAN: Because you're crazy. You do nutty, wild things all the time.

LUCKY: That doesn't sound like me.

CLARK: Are you kidding? That is exactly like you.

LUCKY: Where am I? I hate this room.

DAKOTA: Oh my God, I'm getting really upset now.

VIVIAN: Me, too. Clark, can we leave you here with him for a minute? We'll be right back. Promise, Lucky! We'll be right back.

DAKOTA: We just need to take this in.

(DAKOTA and VIVIAN exit.)

CLARK: What don't you like about this room?

LUCKY: Clark, right?

CLARK: Right! You remember!

LUCKY: Well, you told me four hundred times already.

CLARK: Right.

LUCKY: Clark, I feel really bad. I don't remember anything.

CLARK: It's OK. We'll remind you.

LUCKY: So why is this my room? Why is it like this?

CLARK: Well, you love the color green. So that's why the walls are green. You also love wrestling. So that's why the posters are on the wall.

LUCKY: What else should I know about myself? I know people are going to ask me stuff, and I just don't know what to say. I can see that they feel bad when I don't know things.

CLARK: Let's see. Well, for starters, we're best friends. Have been for a while now. We've always gone to school together. At first, when we were really little, you used to pick on me. But now you don't. You stopped when I punched you in the face when we were seven. We were friends from then on. I guess you respected me then. Now . . . you could say we're sort of . . . well, we're cool in our own way. We have lots of friends, you know, people who talk to us. You especially are friendly with everyone.

LUCKY: So we're dorks.

CLARK: Yes and no. We're not in band or the audio-visual club, but we're not jocks or popular or anything.

LUCKY: We're untalented dorks.

CLARK: I guess you could say so. People think you're sort of goofy. And I just tag along a little. I'm more shy, I guess, and you're the outgoing one. So, as you can tell, you tend to do kinda goofy stuff to get people to look at you. I guess maybe you're a little insecure or something? And you like Leigh, that girl who was in the gym earlier today. You've liked her for a long time.

LUCKY: Does she like me?

CLARK: Not really. I don't think she *hates* you, but, uh . . .

LUCKY: I'm a dork.

CLARK: You do annoy her a little.

LUCKY: So why am I called Lucky?

CLARK: Your mom called you that. It's because you've never broken a bone and you're always doing crazy things.

LUCKY: So what do I want to be when I'm older?

CLARK: You want to be a wrestler.

LUCKY: You're kidding. I want to be a wrestler?

CLARK: Totally! You'll wrestle anyone, anywhere, anytime.

LUCKY: I like wrestling.

CLARK: More than life itself!

LUCKY: Wrestling is when two grown men dressed in short shorts grab each other and groan and throw each other on the ground?

CLARK: That's it!

LUCKY: And I like that? More than anything?

CLARK: You don't remember? I thought at least you'd remember that.

LUCKY: Clark, can I be straight with you?

CLARK: Yeah. We are best friends.

LUCKY: I don't know that I'm going to be the same person anymore. The person I was. I don't know. It's been two weeks, and I still don't remember anything. And I just don't feel the same. I look around me, I look at this room, and I think, "What was I thinking!" Know what I mean? This stuff doesn't mean anything to me. I can't imagine why I wanted it. Why I liked it. So . . . I'm just worried . . . I mean, maybe I will be the same. But maybe I won't. I think it's possible . . . you might be disappointed in me. Everyone might be. I can see we were best friends. It sounds like we had a lot of fun over the years. But it's all gone. I can't remember any of it. So I might not be so crazy anymore. I might not be fun. I don't think I'll be wrestling or jumping off of stuff anymore. I just hope that people will forgive me and still like me if I'm not what they want me to be. I don't want to let anyone down.

CLARK: Don't worry about it. Besides, you might get your memory back. Who knows?

LUCKY: I guess it's possible. But if my memory never comes back and if maybe . . .

CLARK: You don't like me anymore.

LUCKY: I don't know. **It's not that I don't like you, it's that I don't think I'm like you. I don't think we have things in common anymore. Whoever I was—I'm not that person anymore.**

CLARK: Know what?

LUCKY: What?

CLARK: **I'm not sure you ever liked me. Not really. I think we were friends mostly because no one else liked us. And—this is really weird—but I don't know that I like this stuff either. I kind of went along with the wrestling thing because you did. I'm not exactly an athlete. And it is sort of strange. But we did have a lot of fun. You were totally obsessed. I liked being around someone who's more friendly than me, you know? I have a hard time with that. Especially around girls. And I didn't have to think much around you either. You made most of the decisions. So you made that kind of stuff a lot easier. Plus, you were so loud that I seemed sort of normal in comparison! So, I don't know . . . Maybe this is a good thing for me, too, us sort of doing our own thing. I mean, it's not good at all because now I don't have a best friend, but maybe I can work out what my interests are. The bad part about being your friend is that there was never any room for disagreement. Things always had to go your way. That part wasn't any good. So, anyway . . . I guess I'll go now.**

LUCKY: Well, you don't have to go. Maybe—this is dumb,

but maybe the new you will get along with the new me. Maybe not. But maybe.

CLARK: We could see. Maybe we could still get along.

LUCKY: Did I really like that girl Leigh? She seems like a know-it-all.

CLARK: She is a little. I think you liked her because she didn't like you, if that makes any sense.

LUCKY: What a dork!

(VIVIAN and DAKOTA enter.)

DAKOTA: Sorry about that.

VIVIAN: You two seem to be getting along!

CLARK: We're OK. But I guess I should go now.

VIVIAN: OK, Clark. See you later.

CLARK: Maybe.

DAKOTA: Would you like some cheddar soup, Lucky?

LUCKY: Cheddar soup?

DAKOTA: It's your favorite.

LUCKY: Sounds disgusting.

VIVIAN: It is.

TALK BACK!

1. Do you ever show off and do nutty things? If so, why? If not, what do you think of people like that?

2. What should you do if someone likes you (as a friend or a girlfriend/boyfriend), but you don't like him or her?

3. You want someone to notice you (like Lucky wants Leigh to notice him). What should you do?

4. Have you ever pretended to like something to go along with a friend? Why or why not?

5. What's the difference between compromising with a friend and being used by someone?

6. Have you ever had a friend change completely? Have you ever wanted to break away from a friendship? What were those experiences like?

THE BOX

5F , 5M

WHO

FEMALES   MALES

April   Bud

Joss   Erik

Sienna   Ken

Felicity   Egan

Kali   Gil

WHERE   Outside school.

WHEN   Present day.

If you don't think you're like your character (or you don't like his or her actions), be careful not to judge him or her. Instead, try to think of why your character would act as he or she does. Are there any circumstances where you might do the same thing? Try asking other people their viewpoint, too. They might have some ideas you never considered.

In Shakespeare's comedy *Twelfth Night*, a know-it-all character gets tricked in a similar fashion. Write a play that centers around a cruel joke. Try to get inside the heads of your characters and figure out why they do what they do.

Scene 1: Enough

(A large wooden box or trunk sits upstage.)

SIENNA: Ken, could you do something for me?

KEN: Sure!

SIENNA: Could you stop following me?

(KEN exits.)

JOSS: That was a little mean.

SIENNA: He won't go away.

FELICITY: But he means well.

KALI: But he's annoying.

FELICITY: True.

APRIL: Here he comes again.

(KEN enters with a flower.)

KEN: Sorry I bugged you.

SIENNA: I guess it's OK.

KALI: Ken, can I ask you something?

KEN: Sure.

KALI: Why do you keep coming back for more? She doesn't like you.

KEN: I know. But I like her. So I don't see why I should hide it.

JOSS: But she doesn't like you. Why do you put yourself through it?

APRIL: We're just trying to help you here.

KEN: But I don't mind. It doesn't bother me.

SIENNA: Do you think I'll change my mind?

KEN: You might.

SIENNA: I won't.

KEN: You might. You never know!

KALI: She knows!

KEN: Never say never. That's my motto.

FELICITY: Stop torturing yourself!

KEN: It's not torture.

APRIL: It should be!

KEN: But it's not!

JOSS: Why not?

KEN: I don't know. I just don't take it that personally. I like Sienna. I know that, you know that, everyone knows that. I think she's cute. I think I have a lot to offer. And I'm terrible at pretending stuff. So I just show it. So I hang around and I get a little annoying sometimes. So what? Everyone's annoying sometimes. And who knows? Maybe one day Sienna will see my good qualities. But she won't as long as I stay away. Therefore, I hang around. It makes perfect sense to me.

SIENNA: But I always say no. I don't like you. I'll always say no. Forever and ever, Ken, the answer will be no. I'm serious. Don't you believe me?

KEN: You can't know how you'll feel forever. No one can. You might change your mind.

SIENNA: I won't!

KEN: You don't have to get mad at me. It's a compliment. At least, I think so. I wouldn't mind it at all if someone liked me. I would think it was nice that someone admired me even if I didn't like them back. It's a compliment! How can that be a bad thing?

SIENNA: Ken, I've been trying to be nice to you for a long time. Really. I don't want to hurt your feelings, but you just don't get it. You just will not listen, no matter what I say. And I can't take it anymore, so I have to say this. You're annoying. I hate being followed. I hate feeling like you're looking at me. I don't like your looks or your voice. I'm sure someone will. But I don't. I don't know why, I just don't. And I really, honestly can't change how I feel. I just— You're—It feels like you're stalking me. I don't like feeling like I'm being followed and watched. That time you came to my house—I didn't like it! It was creepy! It made me feel like you were staring into my bedroom window. I like privacy, I don't like you, and I don't want you around!

KEN: But I wasn't staring at you or trying to scare you. I won't do that anymore.

SIENNA: Don't do any of it, Ken. Just go away. Just leave me alone. I'm not the girl for you. You need to find someone who actually likes you.

KEN: But I like you.

SIENNA: Who cares!

JOSS: Give it up, Ken.

KALI: Seriously. It's over, Ken.

APRIL: You're scaring her.

KEN: Well, just take this flower.

SIENNA: I don't want your stupid flower!

KEN: OK! Calm down. I'm not going to molest you or anything. I'm just trying to be nice.

SIENNA: I know, but—

KEN: I'll go now. Jeez. You shouldn't be so full of yourself. I might be the only guy who likes you, you know. You don't know. You might have blown something good, Sienna.

(KEN exits.)

SIENNA: He drives me nuts! I can't stand him! Was I too mean? I didn't mean to be cruel, but he just won't take no for an answer!

APRIL: It's OK.

KALI: He needs to drop dead.

FELICITY: Well, he needs to understand you don't like him.

SIENNA: I had to do it, right?

JOSS: His feelings were hurt. I bet you broke his heart.

APRIL: But he needed to hear it.

SIENNA: He really does make me nervous.

   (GIL, ERIK, EGAN, and BUD enter.)

GIL: Who makes you nervous?

SIENNA: Oh, it's nothing.

KALI: Ken.

ERIK: He's a weird kid.

FELICITY: He loves Sienna.

ERIK: I know!

EGAN: Everyone knows! It's, like, his mission in life.

SIENNA: It's creepy!

BUD: Is he bothering you?

SIENNA: Well . . .

KALI: Yes.

JOSS: He's just trying to get her to like him.

BUD: But that's not right. You can't go around scaring and bugging people to get them to like you.

GIL: Well, it doesn't make sense. Otherwise, celebrities would be dating their fans. It just doesn't work like that.

ERIK: If only it did!

EGAN: Who would you go after, Erik?

BUD: Hey! Let's stick to the subject here. So you don't like Ken and he's bugging you.

SIENNA: I guess.

ERIK: Yes or no?

SIENNA: Well, yes.

BUD: So we should help her.

EGAN: What can we do?

GIL: The box.

JOSS: What?

GIL: *(Pointing at the box onstage.)* The box!

APRIL: What about it?

ERIK: Put him in the box! Great idea!

JOSS: But that's a little cruel.

KALI: Come on, Joss. He deserves it.

FELICITY: For how long?

EGAN: A day.

JOSS: A whole day?

SIENNA: I don't know . . .

BUD: Do you want him to leave you alone or not?

KALI: Yes. Right, Sienna?

SIENNA: Yes.

BUD: Consider it done.

EGAN: How are we going to get him in there?

ERIK: We could push him in.

GIL: What about Sienna?

FELICITY: What about her?

GIL: He would do anything for her, right?

ERIK: Right . . .

GIL: So if she wants him in a box, he'll get in a box.

JOSS: He's not that dumb.

GIL: No, seriously, he will! If we tell him it's her test to prove his love . . .

APRIL: Won't his parents wonder where he is?

ERIK: We'll just tell him that he has to prove himself to Sienna tonight. Tell him to tell his parents he won't be home.

BUD: He'll be so excited; he'll do whatever we say!

JOSS: But it's mean!

BUD: Get over it, Joss. It's the only way he'll stop.

Scene 2: Inside and Outside

(The box is in the same place. JOSS and EGAN's conversation takes place as far from the box as possible.)

JOSS: How long has it been?

EGAN: Well, since six o'clock last night.

JOSS: It's four in the afternoon!

EGAN: So?

JOSS: So it's been . . . what? Twenty-two hours!

EGAN: I know.

JOSS: Shouldn't we let him out?

EGAN: Soon.

JOSS: Hasn't he . . . hasn't he been hungry?

EGAN: Yeah.

JOSS: So?

EGAN: He's not going to die or anything.

JOSS: Isn't he uncomfortable? It must be awful in there. What about . . . hasn't he had to go to the bathroom?

EGAN: I don't know.

(BUD and ERIK enter.)

JOSS: This is sick. I'm stopping this now.

EGAN: No!

(BUD grabs JOSS.)

BUD: I don't think so, Joss.

JOSS: This is wrong, Bud! You're not supposed to be cruel to other people. This is just basically wrong. I don't care who you are or what your religion is or anything, this is just not right. Maybe this sounds stupid to you, but you're supposed to be nice to other people. Just because Ken is a little . . . OK, well, he's a kind of a geek and a loser and a little weird, but that doesn't give us the right to do whatever we want to him. He really didn't do anything bad. So he annoyed Sienna. Big deal! His intentions were good. He likes her. So we're punishing him because he goes about showing it in a way that's not . . . appropriate? Don't you see how this doesn't make sense, you guys? Think about it. And think about what this is doing to him. Does the punishment fit the crime? Personally, I really, really think this has gone too far. Don't do this anymore. Please. Stop this before it gets any worse. Do we even know if he's OK?

KEN: *(From inside the box.)* Is someone there?

JOSS: Let go of me, Bud! I'm letting him out!

BUD: Just a little while longer!

KEN: Can you please let me out? I don't want to be here anymore. I . . . I know Sienna wants me to do this, but

. . . I tried and I just can't take this anymore. Please? Is anyone there?

JOSS: Bud, let him out. Come on, guys. This is torture.

ERIK: Do you like him, Joss?

JOSS: No! I just think this is wrong. You shouldn't do this to anyone.

ERIK: You like him!

JOSS: I don't! He said he didn't like Sienna anymore. So we should let him out.

EGAN: He didn't say that. He just said he wanted to get out.

ERIK: He'll probably stalk you next. But I guess you'd like that, Joss.

JOSS: Just let him out.

(EGAN, BUD, and ERIK surround JOSS.)

BUD: No, Joss.

JOSS: Fine.

(JOSS exits.)

ERIK: Girls are wusses.

(GIL enters.)

GIL: What's up with Joss?

EGAN: She feels sorry for Ken.

GIL: How's he doing?

(BUD knocks on the top of the box.)

BUD: Hey! How are ya doing in there?

KEN: Let me out!

ERIK: Not yet!

KEN: Please!

EGAN: Sienna's not going to like this attitude.

GIL: Are you sure you don't want to stay in there anymore?

KEN: Yes!

BUD: You don't know what you're saying, Ken. You have a chance to win your dream girl here. You know, Sienna told me she secretly liked you. *(Beat.)* Can you hear me, Ken? Sienna told me that for real. That she liked you. She said you just intimidated her. Since you came on so strong.

(FELICITY enters and stands off to the side, unseen by the boys.)

BUD: She wasn't sure if you really, really meant all those mushy things you said to her. Then she thought of this. A way for you to prove yourself. To prove your love, Ken. Because we all know you're in love with her. You haven't made that a secret.

(Beat.) Sienna told me just today, Ken, that she wants to give herself body and soul to a guy who really, really cares for her and would do anything—anything!—for her. Are you that guy, Ken? Is it worth it to you? Because we'll let you out. Just say so, Ken, and we'll open this box. But then Sienna would know that you don't really care. She would know that you're really not the guy for her. What's it going to be, Ken? *(Beat.)* That's what I thought.

(Beat.)

FELICITY: I thought the point of this was to *stop* Ken from liking Sienna.

BUD: Sure.

FELICITY: You're doing the opposite.

ERIK: Maybe.

FELICITY: Joss was right. You're enjoying this.

EGAN: You think this is fun? This is babysitting.

FELICITY: I do think you're having fun. I think you're having a lot of fun.

GIL: Give me a break.

FELICITY: Gil, you weren't in math class today. Were you out here?

GIL: Maybe. So?

FELICITY: So I think you've all been out here torturing him at every opportunity.

EGAN: We had to make sure he stayed in the box.

ERIK: Sometimes he'd make a lot of noise. We'd have to shut him up or we'd get in trouble.

FELICITY: Let him out.

BUD: No.

FELICITY: Let him out or I'll tell.

BUD: You'll get in trouble, too.

FELICITY: I don't care. Besides, Joss will back me up. We'll say we had nothing to do with it.

EGAN: We can say the same thing.

FELICITY: Who is the principal going to believe? You guys or us? I think she'll believe us.

GIL: Come on, Felicity. You wouldn't.

FELICITY: I would.

(Beat.)

BUD: No way.

FELICITY: Fine.

(FELICITY exits.)

EGAN: What if she tells?

BUD: She won't.

GIL: She might.

BUD: She won't!

ERIK: Maybe we should let him out.

(FELICITY, JOSS, APRIL, KALI, and SIENNA enter.)

JOSS: Let him out now!

SIENNA: I think this has gone too far. I think we should stop.

KALI: I don't think we really thought this through. I was just thinking about . . . it must really hurt to be in there.

FELICITY: See? Even Kali thinks so.

APRIL: Please, open the box.

ERIK: It's been almost twenty-four hours.

SIENNA: I appreciate what you tried to do—

FELICITY: But they didn't, Sienna!

KALI: It doesn't matter. Just do it. Open the box.

(Long beat. No one moves. Eventually, BUD walks over to the box and opens it.)

BUD: Get out, buddy!

KEN: I thought you were Buddy.

BUD: Right. That's my name.

KEN: Oh.

APRIL: Are you OK, Ken?

KEN: I don't know. I just . . .

   (KEN smiles.)

ERIK: Are you happy, Ken?

KEN: What?

JOSS: Are you OK?

KEN: OK?

SIENNA: He's acting weird.

KALI: Even for him.

FELICITY: We should get him home.

EGAN: What if he tells his parents?

GIL: Ken, what are you going to tell your parents?

KEN: I'm tired. The sun is so bright!

BUD: See? We're fine.

JOSS: Until he remembers.

BUD: If he threatens to tell, we'll put him in the box again.

APRIL: You're sick, Bud.

BUD: Am I?

GIL: I think you might be.

BUD: No more than the rest of you.

TALK BACK!

1. Could this happen at your school? Why or why not?

2. What else could Sienna do to get Ken to leave her alone?

3. Was Ken nice or creepy? What advice would you give him?

4. Have you ever liked someone who didn't like you? How did you handle it?

5. What do you think it was like for Ken being in that box?

6. What might be the long-term effects of this experience for Ken?

7. Which character is most sympathetic in this play? Who is the least sympathetic? Why?

DIFFERENT

4F , 4M

WHO

FEMALES   MALES
   Audrey   Gary
   Scarlett   Jake
   Patricia   Oz
   Tatiana   Scott

WHERE School.

WHEN Present day.

🎭 If you're ever rehearsing and things start to feel stale, try doing these two things: (1) Take one aspect of your character's personality and pump it way up (if you're happy, be *really* happy) and (2) act out your character the complete opposite way of how you think it ought to be done. It keeps things fun and sometimes you can discover new things about your character you might not have considered otherwise.

✎ Your main character can change physical shape at will. When would it be useful? When might having this superpower be a problem? Write a play with this structure: (1) give the character an assignment where the superpower must be used, (2) see the power being used, (3) put the character in an awkward situation due to the power.

Scene 1: Flat Pat

SCARLETT: Hi, everybody! I'm here! Let the fun begin!

AUDREY: Scarlett! I have so much to tell you. I had the best summer.

TATIANA: Audrey had this cute guy kiss her. Or so she says!

AUDREY: It's true! He was way cute, too.

PATRICIA: Is he dead now?

SCARLETT: Shut up, Patty.

AUDREY: Yeah, shut up, Patty. Don't bring me down. I'm in love!

PATRICIA: But you're not going to see him anymore.

AUDREY: No, but so what?

SCARLETT: Did anyone else get kissed?

TATIANA: I want to hear Audrey's details!

SCARLETT: So I guess you didn't.

TATIANA: Maybe I did.

SCARLETT: Get out, Tatiana! Don't tell me you did, too.

TATIANA: Well, it was terrible.

AUDREY: So what! Oh my God, we have so much to talk

about! I don't even have to ask about you, Scarlett. We could probably spend hours talking about you and Mark.

PATRICIA: Who's Mark?

AUDREY: Only Scarlett's true love! She's been writing me about him all summer.

TATIANA: How romantic, Scarlett!

AUDREY: How come you believe her and not me?

TATIANA: You exaggerate.

PATRICIA: Doesn't anyone want to know about my summer?

SCARLETT: Of course! We just need to get up-to-date on our love lives first.

PATRICIA: What makes you think I don't have a love life?

AUDREY: You have a love life, Patricia?

PATRICIA: Well, no, but you didn't know that until just now.

TATIANA: Yes, but, Patty—You're not exactly the type. We could guess.

PATRICIA: What do you mean I'm not the type?

SCARLETT: Are you kidding, Patty? Sometimes it's hard to tell.

PATRICIA: I'm not kidding at all.

AUDREY: Patty Pat, you've never been that into boys.

PATRICIA: Well, I'm not boy crazy, but it doesn't mean I don't like them. I might. I could.

SCARLETT: Of course you could. We're just saying you're not a goofball like the rest of us about all this.

TATIANA: You're our rock, Patty. Without you, the rest of us would just float off into total unreality.

PATRICIA: Thanks a lot.

AUDREY: It's a compliment!

SCARLETT: You should have been kissed this summer, Patty. By a really hot guy! What would Patty's guy be like?

TATIANA: Smart, funny . . .

AUDREY: Sarcastic, geeky—in a good way . . .

SCARLETT: I bet he'd wear glasses and be skinny.

PATRICIA: Because I wear glasses and I'm skinny?

SCARLETT: Just because. That's what I see.

PATRICIA: Well, I guess it doesn't make any difference because I spent the summer watching TV and eating Doritos.

TATIANA: I wish I could eat Doritos and stay skinny.

AUDREY: Don't we all. You're so lucky, Patty.

PATRICIA: I don't feel lucky. I'd rather be kissed and be big as a house.

SCARLETT: Unfortunately, I don't think those things go together!

PATRICIA: Well, they should! You guys, I hate to bring down the mood, but can I be serious for a second?

AUDREY: Sure. What is it?

PATRICIA: What's wrong with me? Seriously. Don't be nice. Be honest, please. I want to know what it is about me that makes it entirely impossible to see me as a kissable girl. I mean, you guys didn't even think to ask me about whether I'd met any guys this summer. And the fact is, before you apologize or anything, you were right. I had a boring summer. I'm invisible. If any guy notices me at all, it's as a sister or something. I know I'm not as . . . flirty or girlie as some other girls, but it doesn't mean I'm dead or anything. I'm just really sick of never getting any attention. No one really sees me as female. I'm like an It. Neutral. What's the word? Neuter. Like a sponge. And I don't want to be someone else exactly; I like who I am. But that makes it even worse. Because it seems like if I'm me, I'm doomed. I don't know what to do. Help me out!

AUDREY: Patty Pat, don't be like that! You're great! We all think you're great.

PATRICIA: Well, you're not boys.

TATIANA: That's true. We're not!

PATRICIA: But you must know something about this. Because you're all obviously much better at this guy stuff than me.

(Beat.)

PATRICIA: Come on, guys, be honest.

SCARLETT: Well, I can think of one thing.

PATRICIA: What's that?

SCARLETT: You . . . You're very smart. And sarcastic. And that might scare guys.

TATIANA: But she can't stop being smart.

AUDREY: Yeah, it would be terrible for her to play dumb or something.

SCARLETT: I agree! But . . . Being sort of sarcastic and negative might make guys think she would reject them. Guys are really chickens. I think they like girls who are really nice. Like Audrey here. She's always really up and sweet. It's just how she is. So a guy, like the guy this summer, probably knew that even if he was a lousy kisser or ugly—

AUDREY: He was cute!

SCARLETT: I know, I know! I'm just saying that Audrey would never be mean about it. But you might.

PATRICIA: No, I wouldn't! Why does everyone think I'm negative? I'm just honest.

SCARLETT: Do you see what I mean, though? I'm not saying you *are* mean, Pat, I'm just saying you could *seem* that way if someone doesn't know you well. And I don't really know what you do about that. 'Cause you are who you are. And you're not Audrey. You're you! And you shouldn't have to act another way. When you meet a guy who's right for you, he'll like that you're smart and sarcastic. Maybe you just need to be more patient. I know this sounds like a cheesy TV show, but I swear that I mean it! You'll meet somebody soon, Patty. And that guy will be great. And he'll like sitting on the couch and eating Doritos and reading books as much as you do.

PATRICIA: I sound like such a loser. Maybe I should try being totally different. How bad could it be? I'm smart, right, so I should be able to pull it off.

AUDREY: But that's so *wrong*, Patty.

TATIANA: I think we're ignoring one obvious thing, guys.

SCARLETT: What's that?

TATIANA: Are you sure you want us to be honest, Patty?

PATRICIA: Well, yeah. But I'm a little scared now.

TATIANA: Well, it's not that bad. It's good in some ways. It's just that . . . well, we could dress you more girlie.

PATRICIA: So I look like a man.

TATIANA: No! That's not what I mean! You know that's not what I mean.

PATRICIA: No, it's true. I'm skinny and flat as a board and I look like a boy.

TATIANA: I just meant you could wear a dress instead of jeans sometimes.

PATRICIA: But that's what I was thinking. I look too much like a boy. Maybe I should get plastic surgery.

AUDREY: You can't get plastic surgery. You're a kid!

TATIANA: Not to mention the money it costs!

SCARLETT: Not to mention you don't need it!

PATRICIA: Sure I do. Martina Margotopolous got a nose job last year.

AUDREY: Yeah, but . . . she's not you.

SCARLETT: Your nose is really cute!

PATRICIA: I wasn't thinking about my nose.

TATIANA: You definitely don't need liposuction.

SCARLETT: Patty, you can't seriously mean . . .

PATRICIA: I want to look like a *woman*, know what I mean?

SCARLETT: You're perfect as you are, Patty!

TATIANA: You really do sound like a mom today, Scarlett!

SCARLETT: Shut up!

AUDREY: I've got an idea.

PATRICIA: I'm almost sorry I asked.

AUDREY: We should ask a guy.

PATRICIA: No way!

AUDREY: Come on! If you want to know how guys think, ask a guy! Here comes Jake.

(JAKE enters.)

TATIANA: I'm not sure this is a good—

AUDREY: Jake!

JAKE: Hey.

AUDREY: Hey. Tell me something, Jake. What do guys look for in girls?

JAKE: What do you mean?

AUDREY: Let me give you some options. Intelligence, humor, hair color—

JAKE: Hair color is somewhat important.

SCARLETT: Hair color? Which is best then?

JAKE: Well, I guess it depends on the girl.

TATIANA: So it's not hair color at all.

JAKE: I guess not. It's, I don't know, the whole girl, I guess.

PATRICIA: So what about . . . size.

JAKE: What do you mean?

PATRICIA: I mean . . . *size.*

JAKE: Tall or short?

PATRICIA: No.

JAKE: Short or fat?

PATRICIA: No. I mean, um, straight or . . . curvy. Know what I mean?

JAKE: I guess.

PATRICIA: So?

JAKE: I guess . . . more . . . curvy.

AUDREY: Really? That actually matters?

SCARLETT: Well, of course it matters, but not everyone likes the same thing, right, Jake?

JAKE: No, I think that's what most guys think. All really. I guess there are some—

PATRICIA: Great! Just great! Thanks a lot, Jake. Thanks!

JAKE: You're welcome.

Scene 2: Patty Hotcakes

(PATRICIA enters. She has stuffed her bra—a lot.)

PATRICIA: Hi, Scott.

SCOTT: Hi.

PATRICIA: How are you?

SCOTT: Fine.

PATRICIA: So . . . notice anything different about me?

SCOTT: Like what?

PATRICIA: I don't know. Like anything . . . physically different?

SCOTT: Um . . . no.

PATRICIA: No?

SCOTT: No.

PATRICIA: Not even if you look very closely?

SCOTT: No.

PATRICIA: You look very nice today, by the way.

SCOTT: Thanks, I guess.

PATRICIA: How do I look?

SCOTT: You look fine.

PATRICIA: Fine?

SCOTT: Yeah.

PATRICIA: I'm wearing a dress.

SCOTT: Yeah. I guess so.

PATRICIA: You "guess so"? It's factual.

SCOTT: I see you're wearing a dress.

PATRICIA: Well— You really don't notice anything different?

SCOTT: No. Should I?

PATRICIA: No. I guess not.

SCOTT: Can I go now?

PATRICIA: I'm not keeping you.

(AUDREY and TATIANA enter.)

AUDREY: So?

PATRICIA: So he didn't even notice.

AUDREY: I still think just wearing the dress is enough.

PATRICIA: They need to be bigger.

TATIANA: Bigger? They're already huge.

PATRICIA: He didn't even notice! Let's go to the bathroom.

TATIANA: It takes so long to get them even! Just leave it alone, Patricia.

PATRICIA: No. If I'm going to try this, I want to try it completely. I'm going to be perky, have a great attitude, and have really huge . . . assets.

AUDREY: Come on then. Let's just get it over with.

(AUDREY, TATIANA, and PATRICIA start to exit. GARY enters.)

GARY: Hi!

AUDREY: Hi!

GARY: Hey, Patty . . . You look . . . really different! Really, really different. Really, really, really different!

PATRICIA: Thanks, Gary!

GARY: You just look so different!

TATIANA: Right, right, right. She looks different.

AUDREY: But how does she look different?

TATIANA: Don't ask him that! Come on, we only have ten minutes to fix them.

(AUDREY, TATIANA, and PATRICIA exit.)

GARY: Fix them? They need fixing?

(OZ and JAKE enter.)

OZ: Gary!

GARY: Have you seen Patty Winslow?

OZ: You mean today?

GARY: Yeah!

OZ: No.

JAKE: Neither have I. You looking for her?

GARY: No, I saw her!

SCOTT: So?

GARY: You gotta see her!

OZ: How come?

JAKE: Patty Winslow?

GARY: Yeah. She's . . . different.

(SCOTT enters.)

GARY: Scott! Have you seen Patty Winslow?

SCOTT: Yeah.

GARY: Doesn't she look different?

SCOTT: **Did she get you to ask me that? Look, I don't know what the point is here, if this is a joke or** something, but I give up, OK? She's . . . bigger, OK? Is that what you want to hear? I noticed, all right? She has a really large chest now. I'm not blind. I can see.

OZ: So what did she do?

SCOTT: How am I supposed to know? What am I— psychic? It just grew overnight. I don't know how these things happen. I'm a guy. I mean, what does she want? You're not supposed to look at them, right? Then she asks me what's different about her. What am I supposed to say? I can't win here. I'm supposed to notice, but not supposed to notice. And what words do you use anyhow? There's a whole other problem. So I try to be polite and re-spectful and what do I get? She gets mad at me. I really don't get women!

(SCARLETT enters.)

SCARLETT: Hi, guys. Scott, have you seen Patty?

SCOTT: I noticed, OK! I noticed! What do you people want from me!

(SCOTT exits.)

SCARLETT: What's wrong with him?

JAKE: I don't know. He went nuts.

OZ: Something about Patty.

SCARLETT: Oh, she didn't!

OZ: What?

SCARLETT: Nothing. Which way did she go?

(GARY points. SCARLETT exits.)

JAKE: Is it me or is everybody nuts lately?

(PATRICIA enters. Her chest is mammoth.)

PATRICIA: Hi, guys!

OZ: Whoa. You *are* different.

GARY: Are they . . . bigger?

JAKE: Are they growing right now?

(OZ gets down to take a closer look.)

OZ: Weird! Are they going to stop or are they, like, going to take over the world?

(GARY gives OZ a shove.)

GARY: Even *I* know not to do that!

OZ: Oh. Sorry.

PATRICIA: So. How are you guys?

JAKE: Good, I guess.

PATRICIA: Really? Wow. What's new?

OZ: Not much.

PATRICIA: Oh my God! Get out! That's so amazing.

GARY: Well, it's not really amazing.

PATRICIA: Sure it is! You guys are so funny!

(SCOTT enters.)

JAKE: OK. This is getting a little weird.

OZ: You're *really* different.

PATRICIA: Thanks, you guys! You're the best!

(SCOTT walks over to PATRICIA.)

SCOTT: Patty, can I talk to you for a sec?

PATRICIA: Boys! Take it easy! There's enough of Patty to go around!

GARY: I'll say.

(PATRICIA and SCOTT walk away from the group. GARY, OZ, and JAKE exit.)

PATRICIA: What can I do for you, Scott?

SCOTT: For starters, you can stop acting like an idiot.

PATRICIA: What?

SCOTT: I talked to Scarlett.

PATRICIA: About what?

SCOTT: About your . . . growth and your strange behavior.

PATRICIA: I have no idea what you mean. Besides, you said you didn't notice!

SCOTT: I was being polite! I didn't know what to say.

PATRICIA: You should say what you think!

SCOTT: I think this is ridiculous. I don't know why you're doing it. It's not you.

PATRICIA: It is now. Did you see the attention I was getting?

SCOTT: I saw. Oz was looking at you like he'd encountered an alien life form.

PATRICIA: Yeah. A woman.

(SCOTT laughs.)

PATRICIA: What's so funny? This is not funny! Don't laugh at me, Scott.

SCOTT: I'm not laughing at you. Well, I am, but . . . Patricia, I don't like this new you. What was so wrong with you before? At least you seemed human.

PATRICIA: Human and boring.

SCOTT: You're lots of things, but not boring. Now you're brainless and vain. *That's* boring. You look like an alien. Or Barbie. Do you know that if Barbie were real, she'd fall over on her face because she's not proportioned?

PATRICIA: Fascinating. Why do you know that?

SCOTT: I don't know why I know that. Who cares? It's just a weird fact that came into my head somehow. But that's beside the point. The point is you're a freak of nature now!

PATRICIA: Well, thank you. Fortunately, not everyone feels that way.

SCOTT: So, you'd rather be phony than yourself. Very mature. Well, the good part is that after a little while you'll start to believe your act. You'll turn into a brainless airhead soon.

PATRICIA: That's redundant.

SCOTT: What?

PATRICIA: Brainless and airhead mean the same thing.

SCOTT: See? This is the Patty I like.

PATRICIA: Yeah, but you don't *like* me.

SCOTT: See what I mean? You're turning into a brainless airhead already.

TALK BACK!

1. Are girls and guys too obsessed with looks or is it totally justified? Why?

2. If you were going to write down your beliefs, what would you say about plastic surgery? When is it a good idea (if ever) and when is it a bad idea (if ever)?

3. Would you consider changing your looks? Why or why not? What would you change?

4. Would you consider changing an aspect of your personality? Why or why not? What would you change?

5. Should Patty stay on this path or should she go back to the way she was?

6. Do you find change exciting or unpleasant? Why? Is it better to be open to change or is it better when things stay the same? Why?

APPENDIX

CHARACTER QUESTIONNAIRE FOR ACTORS

Fill in the following questionnaire as if you are your character. Make up anything you don't know.

PART 1: The Facts

NAME:

AGE/BIRTHDATE:

HEIGHT:

WEIGHT:

HAIR COLOR:

EYE COLOR:

CITY/STATE/COUNTRY YOU LIVE IN:

GRADE*:

BROTHERS/SISTERS:

PARENTS:

UPBRINGING (strict, indifferent, permissive, etc.):

---

* If you are an adult, what educational level did you reach (college, medical school, high school, etc.)?

PART 2: Rate Yourself

On a scale of 1 to 10 (circle one: 10 = great, 1 = bad), rate your:

APPEARANCE	1 2 3 4 5 6 7 8 9 10
IQ	1 2 3 4 5 6 7 8 9 10
SENSE OF HUMOR	1 2 3 4 5 6 7 8 9 10
ATHLETICISM	1 2 3 4 5 6 7 8 9 10
ENTHUSIASM	1 2 3 4 5 6 7 8 9 10
CONFIDENCE	1 2 3 4 5 6 7 8 9 10
DETERMINATION	1 2 3 4 5 6 7 8 9 10
FRIENDLINESS	1 2 3 4 5 6 7 8 9 10
ARTISTICNESS	1 2 3 4 5 6 7 8 9 10

Do you like yourself?	YES	NO
Do you like your family?	YES	NO
Do you like the opposite sex?	YES	NO
Do you like most people you meet?	YES	NO

Which of the following are important to you and which are not? Circle one.

WEALTH	Important	Not Important
KNOWLEDGE	Important	Not Important
POWER	Important	Not Important
PEACE	Important	Not Important
POPULARITY	Important	Not Important
LIKABILITY	Important	Not Important
LOVE	Important	Not Important
SPIRITUALITY/RELIGION	Important	Not Important

PART 3: Favorites

List your favorites (be specific).

FOOD:

SONG:

BOOK:

MOVIE:

TV SHOW:

CITY:

SEASON:

COLOR:

PIECE OF CLOTHING:

SMELL:

ANIMAL:

SOUND:

SCHOOL SUBJECT:

PLACE:

PERSON (historical or living):

PART 4: Describe Yourself

Circle all words/phrases that apply to you:

SHY	OUTGOING
OUTDOOR TYPE	INDOOR TYPE
POSITIVE	NEGATIVE
PARTY PERSON	COUCH POTATO
HOMEBODY	LEADER
FOLLOWER	MOODY
CALM	SILLY
HAPPY	SAD
RELAXED	ENERGETIC
INTELLECTUAL	CLEVER
NEAT	MESSY
FUNNY	HONEST
SNEAKY	DISHONEST
OPEN-MINDED	JUDGMENTAL
CARING	CREATIVE
PRACTICAL	WILD
CAREFUL	WELL-LIKED
ARTISTIC	LAZY
OPINIONATED	IMAGINATIVE
REALISTIC	DRAMATIC
STREETWISE	TOLERANT
HARD-WORKING	SPONTANEOUS
STRONG	BRAVE
CURIOUS	QUIET
CHATTY	DARK
SUNNY	DISAPPOINTING
HOPEFUL	UNDERSTANDING
KIND	BORED
DIFFICULT	COMPLICATED
SWEET	POWERFUL
MACHO	ENTHUSIASTIC
GIRLY	INSECURE
LUCKY	PICKY
DISADVANTAGED	FRIENDLY
GOSSIPY	ANGRY
SECRETIVE	WISHY-WASHY
INDEPENDENT	GEEKY
WEAK	COOL
NURTURING	ANNOYING
REBELLIOUS	GOOD

PART 5: Truth/Dreams

If I die tomorrow, people will remember me as a:

One thing that really annoys me is:

My worst habit is:

I'm really scared of:

My parents think I'm:

When I grow up, I want to be*:

Superpower I'd most like to have:

The thing I'd most like to change about myself is:

My greatest talent is:

I'd most like to travel to:

Three professions I'd like to try:

The title for the story of my life would be:

* If your character is an adult, what is your character's job and does he or she enjoy it?

PLAYWRIGHT'S CHECKLIST

Does my play have:

☐ Conflict?

If everyone gets along, not much happens! It's important to have conflict in any play, comedy, or drama.

☐ Character development?

Do the characters change at all in the course of the play for better or worse? It's interesting to the audience to see some variety in character. We all act differently in different situations, so it makes sense for a character to become more complex when he or she is faced with conflicts.

☐ Plot twists?

What could be more exciting than being surprised by a plot twist you hadn't expected?

☐ Believable dialogue?

Even if the characters are strange and out-of-this-world, make sure the dialogue sounds something like the way people actually speak to one another. Any character voices you create must remain consistent throughout. For example, if a character is very intellectual and proper, having them say "I ain't gonna go" is going to seem very out of place.

☐ A strong sense of place and time?

Especially when you don't have a big set and costumes, it's important to make the play's setting clear.

☐ Characters you can relate to?

Every play has at least one character the audience can understand and sympathize with. A good way to create conflict is to put this "normal" character in the path of another character that is odd, otherworldly, or downright horrible!

SCENE ELEMENTS WORKSHEET

Answer these questions for each scene you do.

WHO: (Who are you?)

WHERE: (Where are you?)

WHEN: (Is this the past, present, or future? Day or night?)

WHY: (Why are you where you are?)

OBJECTIVE: (What do you want?)

ACTIONS: (What do you do to get what you want? For example, beg, flatter, pressure, and so on.)

CHARACTER TRAITS: (What are you like as a person?)

RELATIONSHIP: (What are your relationships to the other characters?)

OBSTACLES: (What or who stands in the way of your objective?)

EXPLORATION GAMES

Draw a picture of your character(s).

Improvise a scene before the play begins or after it ends.

Dress as your character(s) to see how it changes your behavior.

Make the scene or play into a musical or an opera.

Listen closely to everyone around you during a scene.

Try to make your acting partners respond to your behavior.

Lead with a different body part: in other words, change which part of your body enters the room first and pulls you forward when you walk. Leading with your nose can make you seem pompous, leading with the top of your head can make you seem insecure, etc.

Change the speed/rhythm at which you speak or move.

Decide who you like and who you don't like in the scene; don't be afraid to show it.

Change your volume (whisper or speak out loudly).

Make your voice higher or lower in pitch.

Notice who's taller and who's shorter than you in the scene; let this affect you.

Change your accent.

Sit down with another actor to make up your characters' past lives together.

Do an activity you think your character might do.

Do a chore around the house the way your character might do it.

Write a diary entry, a letter of complaint, or a personal ad as your character.

Come up with a gesture that your character does habitually.

THE AUTHOR

Kristen Dabrowski is an actress, writer, acting teacher, and director. She received her MFA from The Oxford School of Drama in Oxford, England. The actor's life has taken her all over the United States and England. Her other books, published by Smith and Kraus, include *111 Monologues for Middle School Actors Volume 1, The Ultimate Audition Book for Teens 3, 20 Ten-Minute Plays for Teens,* and the *Teens Speak* series. Currently, she lives in the world's smallest apartment in New York City. You can contact the author at monologue madness@yahoo.com.